InDesign® CS
Creating Basic Publications (Level 1 - Windows)

Gary Young

Gary Young is a content developer and trainer. An Adobe® Certified Expert in five products, Gary has been working with publishing, design, and multimedia software for over ten years, and has written several courses that have been used by training companies worldwide. These courses include series of books covering Adobe® InDesign, Photoshop, Illustrator, PageMaker, and Acrobat, as well as QuarkXPress, Macromedia Flash, Fireworks, Director, and FreeHand. He has trained a broad range of clients in the classroom, onsite, and via the Internet, including graphic designers, production teams for advertising agencies, Web designers, and newspaper imaging, layout, and illustration staff.

InDesign® CS: Creating Basic Publications (Level 1 - Windows)

Course Number: 078195
Course Edition: 1.0
For software version: CS

ACKNOWLEDGEMENTS

Project Team

Curriculum Developer and Technical Writer: Gary S. Young • **Copy Editors/Reviewing Editors/Layout Technicians:** Kevin Ogburn and Kirsten Nelson Sitnick

Project Support

Development Manager: Jennifer Hennard

NOTICES

HELP US IMPROVE OUR COURSEWARE

Your comments are important to us. Please contact us at Element K Press LLC, 1-800-478-7788, 500 Canal View Boulevard, Rochester, NY 14623, Attention: Product Planning, or through our Web site at **http://support.elementkcourseware.com.**

InDesign® CS: Creating Basic Publications (Level 1 - Windows)

CONTENT OVERVIEW

CONTENTS

InDesign® CS: Creating Basic Publications (Level 1 - Windows)

Contents

Lesson 1: InDesign® Environment

Lesson 2: Basic Documents

Lesson 3: Master Pages

CONTENTS

CONTENTS

CONTENTS

ABOUT THIS COURSE

Adobe® InDesign® is a robust and easy to use design and layout program. With it you can create documents of many types, from single page advertisements and flyers, to complex multi-page color publications. In this course you will learn the basics of creating documents with InDesign®.

Course Prerequisites

In order to be successful with this course, a basic understanding of the operating system and of using applications in general is needed.

Course Objectives

When you're done working your way through this course, you'll be able to:

*   Identify and use InDesign® environment elements; and navigate through an InDesign® document.

*   Create and modify text and graphic frames; and import text and images from other applications.

*   Use master pages and guides to design a document's layout and to add automatic page numbering; and apply masters to document pages.

*   Import text; thread text throughout a document; reflow text threads; and change the number of columns.

*   Define colors and swatches and apply them to fills and strokes of frames.

*   Apply character formatting; apply paragraph formatting; create styles to streamline formatting; and set text inset spacing.

*   Place and manipulate graphics; control text wrap around graphics; and create and manage layers.

*   Apply transparency effects to native objects and placed images and graphics; and work with Transparency Flattener settings.

*   Create sophisticated tables.

*   Prepare documents for handoff to commercial printers.

*   Create Acrobat PDF files for the Web and for print.

COURSE SETUP INFORMATION

Hardware and Software Requirements

To run this course, you will need:

- An Intel Pentium II, III, or 4 processor.

- Microsoft Windows 2000 (with Service Pack 2), or XP operating system.

- A hard disk with at least 185 MB of available hard disk space to install the InDesign® CS software, and an additional 10 MB of free hard disk space for the course data files.

- At least 128 MB of random-access memory (RAM).

- A CD-ROM drive.

- Monitor resolution of at least 256 colors at 1024 X 768 pixels.

- Adobe® InDesign® CS.

Class Requirements

In order for the class to run properly, perform the procedures described below.

1. On the course CD-ROM, open the 078_195 folder. Then, open the Data folder. Run the 078195dd.exe self-extracting file located within. This will install a folder named 078195Data on your C drive. This folder contains all the data files that you will use to complete this course.

2. In order to ensure that all needed features of InDesign® will be available for this course, run a standard install from the software installation CD. Use the Adobe® InDesign® installation CD to install the Adobe® PS driver.

3. This course will run best if you remove the InDesign® preferences files. If these preferences are not removed, some of the options chosen during previous sessions may affect your work during this course. You can delete the InDesign® preferences files as you launch the application. Press Ctrl+Alt+Shift as you launch InDesign®, and in the dialog box that appears, click Yes to remove the preferences files. After the application launches, choose Window→Workspace→[Default] to return the palettes to their default positions.

4. This course specifies the use of certain fonts. If these fonts are not installed, the documents the student works on will not display as intended. Make sure the fonts Arial, Times New Roman, Verdana, and Webdings are installed on the computer.

   Additionally, make sure that the font Adobe® Garamond Pro is installed. Follow the instructions on the Adobe® InDesign® installation CD (look inside the Adobe® OpenType fonts folder) to install Adobe® Garamond Pro.

5. This course will run most smoothly if your monitor resolution is set to at least 1024 x 768 pixels per inch.

6. Staged data files have been provided with this course. These files will allow you to begin the course at a lesson other than Lesson 1, or could help you find a possible solution if you get stuck at any point during the course. If you wish to use the staged data files, on the course CD-ROM, open the 078_195 folder. Then, open the Data folder. Run the 078195ddstaged.exe self-extracting file located within. This will install a folder named 078195Staged on your C drive.

   In the 078195Staged folder on your C drive, the Lesson folders contain all the course images and data, completed up to the lesson indicated by the folder name. For example, if you would like to begin this course at Lesson 4, you should open the Lesson 4 folder in the 078195Staged folder on your C drive. All the files you'll need to complete the rest of the course are contained in the new folder.

7. In addition to the specific setup procedures needed for this class to run properly, you should also check the Element K Courseware product support Web site at **http://support.elementkcourseware.com** for more information. Any updates about this course will be posted there.

List of Additional Files

Printed with each lesson is a list of files students open to complete the tasks in that lesson. Many tasks also require additional files that students do not open, but are needed to support the file(s) students are working with. These supporting files are included with the student data files on the course CD-ROM or data disk. Do not delete these files.

HOW TO USE THIS BOOK

You can use this book as a learning guide, a review tool, and a reference.

As a Learning Guide

Each lesson covers one broad topic or set of related topics. Lessons are arranged in order of increasing proficiency with *InDesign*® *CS*; skills you acquire in one lesson are used and developed in subsequent lessons. For this reason, you should work through the lessons in sequence.

We organized each lesson into explanatory topics and step-by-step activities. Topics provide the theory you need to master *InDesign*® *CS*, activities allow you to apply this theory to practical hands-on examples.

You get to try out each new skill on a specially prepared sample file. This saves you typing time and allows you to concentrate on the technique at hand. Through the use of sample files, hands-on activities, illustrations that give you feedback at crucial steps, and supporting background information, this book provides you with the foundation and structure to learn *InDesign*® *CS* quickly and easily.

As a Review Tool

Any method of instruction is only as effective as the time and effort you are willing to invest in it. For this reason, we encourage you to spend some time reviewing the book's more challenging topics and activities.

As a Reference

You can use the Concepts sections in this book as a first source for definitions of terms, background information on given topics, and summaries of procedures.

Icons Serve As Cues:

Throughout the book, you will find icons representing various kinds of information. These icons serve as an "at-a-glance" reminder of their associated text.

 Topic:
Represents the beginning of a topic

 Check Your Skills:
Represents a Check Your Skills practice

 Task:
Represents the beginning of a task

 Apply Your Knowledge:
Represents an Apply Your Knowledge activity

 Student Note:
A margin note that highlights information for students

 Glossary Term:
A margin note that represents a definition. This definition also appears in the glossary

 QuickTip:
A margin note that represents a tip, shortcut, or additional way to do something

 Warning:
A margin note that represents a caution; this note typically provides a solution to a potential problem

 Web Tip:
A margin note that refers you to a website where you might find additional information

 Version Note:
A margin note that represents an alternate way to do something using a different version of the software

 Overhead:
In the instructor edition, an overhead note refers to a .ppt slide that the instructor can use in the lesson

 Additional Instructor Note:
A margin note in the instructor's Edition that refers the instructor to more information in the back of the book

 Instructor Note:
A margin note in the Instructor's Edition that gives tips for teaching the class

InDesign® Environment

Overview

InDesign® CS is a robust and easy-to-use layout application. It's powerful enough to produce sophisticated magazine and newspaper layouts, as well as newsletters, brochures, mailers, or any other kind of document you wish to create. It contains many more layout features than in word processing applications, but is still easy to use. Although you can add text and create some graphic elements within InDesign, you will typically use other applications to type large quantities of text and to create, edit, and adjust images. You will then use InDesign to combine text and graphics as you create the layouts you need for your document.

In this lesson, you will learn about the InDesign window, palettes, and tools. You will also learn several techniques for navigating through an InDesign document.

Data Files
Sample Document.indd

Lesson Time
30 minutes

Objectives

To navigate InDesign documents, you will:

1A **Identify InDesign environment elements.**

You will identify and use several of the elements in the document window, and work with palettes and the Toolbox.

1B **Navigate through an InDesign document.**

You will zoom in and out, and move between document pages. You will also use several shortcuts to speed navigating through documents.

 **Topic 1A**

InDesign Environment Elements

InDesign's environment includes menus, palettes, and window elements. You can use the menus, palettes, and window elements to access InDesign commands, tools, and other features to work with document content.

InDesign Window Elements

The InDesign window elements include the pasteboard, guides, Magnification field, page number controls, and palettes.

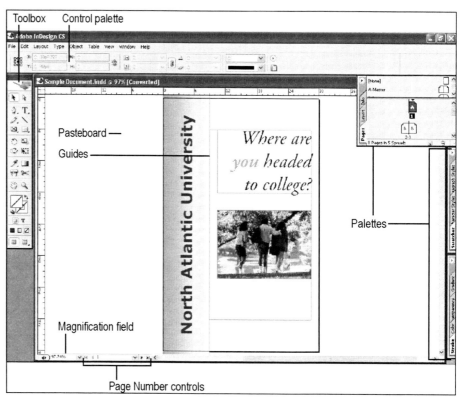

Window Element	Description
Pasteboard	The pasteboard is the area that surrounds the pages of the document. You may store text and images on the pasteboard until you are ready to use them.
Guides	Guides are lines that indicate the position of margins and other areas of the page that you specify. Guides do not print, but they are visible on the screen to help you align elements on document pages.
Magnification field	The Magnification field allows you to view and change the percentage of actual size at which you are viewing the document. You can type a value into the field, or select a magnification from the drop-down list.
Page Number controls	The Page Number controls indicate the page you are currently viewing and allow you to navigate to other pages.
Palettes	InDesign employs several palettes to let you choose tools, view and edit measurements, arrange document pages, choose colors, create lists and indexes, and specify printing parameters.

InDesign Palettes

When you initially launch InDesign, the Toolbox, Control palette, and Pages palette are showing. Most palettes, including the Pages palette, are contained in groups with two or three other palettes. One palette within a group is visible at a time, and you can click a palette's tab to display it within its group. Many palettes appear as tabs grouped along the right side of the screen. You can show any palette by clicking its tab if the tab is visible, or by choosing its name from the Window menu or from the Type menu for those specific to changing text attributes.

If you want a palette that is grouped along the side of the screen to appear as a floating palette, you can drag its tab away from the screen edge. To store a palette as a side tab at the left or right edge of the screen, you can drag its tab to the left or right edge of the screen. You can then click the palette's tab to show or hide its contents. Storing the palettes you use most frequently as side tabs is useful so you can easily access them and can then collapse them to free up your main work area.

Most palettes are stored in groups with several other palettes. Opening one palette in a group opens the whole group. Since you can only view one palette within a palette group at a time, you can drag a palette by its tab to separate it from its palette group so that it can be visible at the same time as other palettes from its former group. You can then drag a palette by its tab, and position the tab next to other palette tabs within a group to add the palette to that group. You can drag palettes or palette groups by their title bars to snap them to the top or bottom of other palettes to position them neatly.

You can hide and show palettes with keyboard shortcuts. You can press Tab to show or hide all palettes. You can hide all palettes except the Toolbox and Control palette by pressing Shift+Tab, or by clicking the Toggle All Palettes Except Toolbox button in the Control palette. The Control palette is a contextual palette whose contents change depending on the currently selected page, content, or tool.

Once you arrange the palettes the way you want, you can save that palette arrangement as a named workspace by choosing Window→Workspace→Save Workspace. This allows you to set up multiple workspaces for the various types of InDesign workflows you use. After saving a workspace, you can select it by choosing from the Window→Workspace submenu.

You can dock a palette by dragging its tab to the bottom of another palette and releasing when a thick black line appears. A docked palette moves with the one it's docked to, and is hidden and shown at the same time. However, unlike grouped palettes, a palette you have docked remains visible at all times; it stays below the original palettes.

TASK 1A-1

Managing Palettes

Objective: To arrange palettes efficiently.

1. **Open the 078195Data folder, then open the Sample folder.**

2. **Double-click the Sample Document.indd icon.** InDesign launches and Sample Document.indd appears.

3. You will experiment with manipulating palettes. You will first close one that you do not need immediately. **Click the Pages palette's tab** to collapse the palette as a side tab.

4. Along the right edge of the screen, **click the Swatches palette tab.** The Swatches palette opens, along with the Paragraph Styles and Character Styles palette tabs.

5. You'll now open a palette that's not already embedded as a side tab. **Choose Window→Navigator.** The Navigator palette appears as a floating palette.

6. **Drag the Navigator palette tab to the left edge of the screen** to embed it as a side tab.

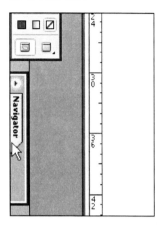

7. **Click in a blank part of the pasteboard to be sure no items are selected.**

8. **Press Tab.** All of the palettes disappear. You can bring them back with the same key.

9. **Press Tab again.** The palettes return. Since you frequently need the Toolbox and the Control palette, you can hide all palettes except them.

10. **Hold down Shift, and press Tab.** All of the palettes except for the Toolbox and Control palette disappear.

11. **Press Tab.** The palettes reappear. You may wish to use these shortcuts to eliminate clutter from your screen as necessary.

Throughout the course, you may want to close palettes you aren't using, then open them when needed.

The Toolbox

The Toolbox, shown in Figure 1-1, contains tools for creating and modifying text frames, graphic frames, lines, and other page elements. A small arrow at the lower right corner of any tool button indicates that additional tools can be accessed by holding down the mouse button on the tool button.

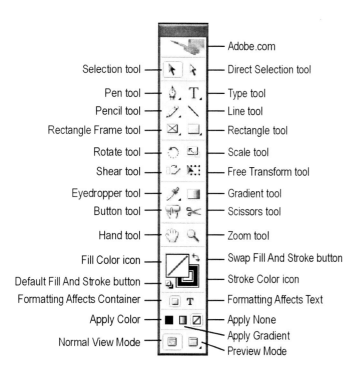

Figure 1-1: *The Toolbox contains tools for creating and modifying text frames, graphic frames, lines, and other page elements.*

Tool	Shortcut	Description
Selection tool	V	Allows you to select and move items, such as text frames and graphic frames.
Direct Selection tool	A	Allows you to move graphics within graphic frames, and to adjust the individual points of frames.
Pen tool	P	Allows you to create additional points along frame paths and to draw and modify *Bézier shapes*. You can choose the Add Anchor Point tool, Delete Anchor Point tool, or Convert Direction Point tool by holding down the mouse button on this tool.
Add Anchor Point tool	=	Allows you to add additional points along a Bézier shape.
Delete Anchor Point tool	–	Allows you to delete points from a Bézier shape.
Convert Direction Point tool	Shift C	Allows you to change sharp corner points on a Bézier shape to smooth curve points or vice versa.

Tool	Shortcut	Description
Type tool	T	Allows you to create and edit text. You can choose the Type On A Path tool from this tool.
Type On A Path tool	Shift T	Allows you to position and edit text along a Bézier shape.
Pencil tool	N	Allows you to draw paths. You can also choose the Smooth tool or Erase tool from this tool.
Smooth tool		Allows you to remove excess angles from an existing Bézier shape.
Erase tool		Allows you to remove a portion of an existing Bézier shape.
Line tool	\	Allows you to create lines on any angle.

Bézier shape:
A line consisting of points connected by curved or straight segments. A Bézier path may be open or closed.

Tool	Shortcut	Description
Rectangle Frame tool	F	Allows you to create rectangular frames that can hold graphics or text. You can also choose the Ellipse Frame tool and Polygon Frame tool from this tool.
Rectangle tool	M	Allows you to create rectangles and squares. You can also choose the Ellipse tool or Polygon tool from this tool.
Ellipse tool	L	Allows you to create ellipses and circles.
Polygon tool		Allows you to create polygons and stars.

You can also hide and show guides and frame edges individually using commands in the View menu. However, Preview Mode also shows the page trimmed to size with any overhanging items shown cut off, so it's a more accurate way to preview your pages for printing.

Tool	Shortcut	Description
Rotate tool	R	Allows you to rotate objects on the page.
Scale tool	S	Allows you to resize objects on the page.
Shear tool	O	Allows you to skew objects by dragging.
Free Transform tool	E	Allows you to perform any transformation to an object using a single tool. Transformations include move, scale, rotate, reflect, or shear.
Eyedropper tool	I	Allows you to copy attributes from type or graphics, then apply those attributes elsewhere.
Gradient tool	G	Allows you to change the angle and length of gradients in gradient-filled shapes.
Button tool	B	Allows you to create buttons for PDF forms.
Scissors tool	C	Allows you to split paths and frames.
Hand tool	H	Allows you to drag the page in a window to scroll it rather than using the scroll bars.
Zoom tool	Z	Allows you to quickly change the magnification to zoom in or out on page areas.
Normal View Mode and Preview Mode	W	Preview Mode hides guides and frame edges, grays the Pasteboard, and shows only the page trim (not any parts that extend from the page onto the Pasteboard), so you can see what your document will look like when printed.

The Toolbox contains the following formatting controls.

Formatting Control	Shortcut	Description
Fill icon	X	Specifies that the next color, gradient, or swatch you apply will affect the fill, or inside, of a frame.
Stroke icon	X	Specifies that the next color, gradient, or swatch you apply will affect the stroke, or surrounding path, of a frame.
Swap Fill & Stroke icon	Shift X	Switches the current fill and stroke colors.
Default Fill & Stroke icon	D	Resets the default fill and stroke (None fill, black stroke) and applies it to any selected objects.
Formatting Affects buttons		Allows you to choose whether a fill and/or stroke applies to the text or its container.
Apply Color button	,	Sets the fill or stroke of the selected object to a solid color.
Apply Gradient button	.	Sets the fill or stroke of the selected object to a gradient.
Apply None button	/	Sets the fill or stroke of the selected object to None, or transparent.

With InDesign, all text and Imported graphics are stored within frames. The primary tools you use to manipulate InDesign elements, such as frames, graphics, and text, are the Selection, Direct Selection, and Type tools. Clicking a frame using the Selection tool selects the frame, displaying selection handles. You can drag from within the frame to move it, or drag the selection handles to resize it. You can also select and move a frame using the Direct Selection tool. However, if you drag a frame's selection handles using the Direct Selection tool, you'll reshape the frame, rather than resize it. The ability to reshape frames allows for great flexibility in conforming text and images to interesting shapes.

If you want to select and modify the text or graphic within a frame, you must use the Type or Direct Selection tools. You can select text using the Type tool, or click within a frame to place an insertion point from which you can type to add text. To select a graphic within a frame, you can click it using the Direct Selection tool. You can then reposition or resize the graphic within its frame. You can use either the Selection or Direct Selection tool to deselect objects.

When you want to move a frame or other object, hold down the mouse for a few moments before dragging the item to obtain a live preview as you drag. Otherwise, you'll only see a bounding box representing the item as you move it.

TASK 1A-2

Manipulating Document Elements

Objective: To use the appropriate tool to manipulate InDesign elements, such as frames, graphics, and text.

Setup: The Sample Document.indd file is open.

1. You will first work with the Selection tool. **Select the Selection tool in the Toolbox.**

2. **Click the picture of the students.** Handles appear at the corners of the frame, indicating that it is selected.

3. **Drag the left middle handle of the frame to the left to slightly overlap the gradient background behind North Atlantic University.** The picture in the frame is larger than the frame itself, so you revealed more of it by enlarging the frame. The frame is acting to crop the picture to size.

4. **Position the Selection tool mouse pointer on the middle of the picture and drag up or down until you're satisfied with its vertical position.** You have resized and moved the frame with the Selection tool.

5. You decide to change the word college to school. **Click the Type tool in the Toolbox.**

6. **Position the mouse pointer to the left of the word college in the text frame above the students.** The mouse pointer appears as an I-beam, indicating that you can select text and position an insertion point for typing.

7. **Drag across the word college to select it, but do not include the ? character.**

8. You can replace the selected text by typing over it. **Type *school*.** The word school replaces college.

9. You will now reposition the picture of the students within its frame. **Click the Direct Selection tool in the Toolbox.**

10. **Click the picture of the students.** You can now see the edges of the original picture.

11. **Drag the picture to move the students roughly to the center of the frame.** The picture moves within the frame, instead of the entire frame moving as it would with the Selection tool. You will now reshape the frame that contains this picture.

12. **Click the edge of the visible picture.** The points that make the frame are selected.

13. **Drag the top left corner point down and to the right into the picture approximately an inch in both directions.** Instead of cropping or resizing the picture while maintaining a rectangular shape, you have changed the shape of the frame. However, you decide to keep the frame rectangular.

14. **Choose Edit→Undo Move.** The frame returns to its rectangular shape.

15. **Click in the pasteboard to the right of the page to deselect all objects.** The handles at the corners of the frame disappear.

Topic 1B

Document Navigation

You can use several methods to view document pages at different magnifications.

- Select commands from the View menu.
- Select preset magnifications from the Magnification drop-down list, or enter custom values in the Magnification field.
- Click or drag using the Zoom tool.

You can use View→Actual Size to display the document at approximately its printed size, although it may not be perfectly accurate depending on the resolution of your monitor. You can use View→Fit On Screen to see the whole page within the current window.

To zoom in on specific areas, you may find the Zoom tool most convenient. You can click the location on the screen you want to zoom in on, or can drag a marquee to designate the area you wish to appear within the window. InDesign can zoom up to 4000% magnification. You can reduce the magnification by holding down Alt as you click or drag with the Zoom tool.

You can also zoom in on a specific object by selecting that object, then zooming using the Magnification drop-down list or field. When no objects are selected, zooming with the Magnification drop-down list or field zooms in on the center of the current page.

TASK 1B-1

Zooming In and Out

Objective: To zoom in and out.

Setup: The Sample Document.indd file is open.

1. You will view the page at actual size to see how large it would print. **Choose View→Actual Size.**

2. **Select the Zoom tool in the Toolbox.**

3. **Click the word North.** The page enlarges on the screen. You will zoom in on the letter A.

4. **Position the Zoom tool mouse pointer just above and to the left of the letter A in the word Atlantic.**

5. **Drag down and to the right to create a marquee around the letter A.**

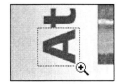

6. **Release the mouse button.** The letter is enlarged and centered in the window.

7. **Hold down Alt.** A - appears in the Zoom tool mouse pointer, indicating that the tool will zoom out.

8. **Click the letter A.** The magnification reduces slightly.

9. **Choose View→Fit Page In Window.** The whole page is visible.

10. **Click the Selection tool in the Toolbox.**

11. **Click the text frame above the picture to select it.** When you zoom in, the selected text frame will be centered in the window.

12. From the Magnification drop-down list at the bottom-left corner of the window, **choose 400%.** The page zooms to 400%, centered on the text frame.

13. You will zoom to 250%. **Double-click in the Magnification field at the bottom left corner of the window to select the value.**

14. **Type *250*, then press Enter.** The document appears at 2½ times actual size, with the text frame in the center of the window.

15. **Choose View→Fit Page In Window.** The whole page is visible again.

Document Navigation

You will use several techniques to move among InDesign document pages. The first method is to use the Pages palette.

The Layout menu contains commands for navigating to the next or previous page or spread, as well as to the first or last page.

The Pages palette displays an icon for each document page, and indicates the placement of each page relative to other pages. For example, the Pages palette indicates whether a document uses facing pages, by displaying icons for facing pages together as a two-page spread. You can double-click a page icon to navigate to that page. When using Fit Spread In Window view, you can double-click the page numbers below the page icons in the Pages palette to center a spread in the window. You can also use the Pages palette's Keep Spreads Together command to create spreads of more than two pages.

Each page is notated with a number below it and a letter on it. The number is the page number, and the letter indicates which master page the document page is based on. The current page appears with an outlined number in the Pages palette.

You can choose to show the page icons in the Pages palette either vertically or horizontally. To change the display, choose Palette Options from the Pages palette drop-down list. You can also change the size of the icons.

You can use the Page controls, shown in Figure 1-2, to go to a page quickly. You can click the page navigation buttons, or can type a page number within the Page field, then press Enter to navigate to that page. In addition, you can select a page number from the Page drop-down list.

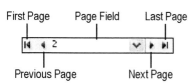

Figure 1-2: *You can navigate directly to specific pages using the Page controls.*

TASK 1B-2

Moving Between Document Pages

Objective: To move from page to page in a document.

Setup: The Sample Document.indd file is open.

1. If the Pages palette is not visible, **click its tab or choose Window→Pages.**

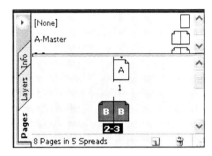

2. **Scroll down in the bottom half of the Pages palette to view the page icons.**

You may want to enlarge the Pages palette so you can see all or most of the page icons at once.

3. **Double-click the letter B on the page 4 icon in the Pages palette.** You are now viewing pages four and five in the document, since they form a spread of facing pages. Page four is centered in the window.

4. **Double-click the letter B on the page 5 icon in the Pages palette.** Page five is centered.

5. **Choose View→Fit Spread In Window.** The spread of pages is centered, rather than one page or the other.

6. **Double-click the page numbers 2-3 beneath the pages two and three icons in the Pages palette.** The pair of pages is centered in the window.

7. At the window's bottom left, **click the Next Page button.** The next page appears in the window.

8. **Click the Previous Page button.** You are now viewing the previous page.

9. **Click the Last Page button.** Page eight appears in the window.

10. **Double-click the page number in the Page field at the bottom of the window.**

11. In the Page Number field, **type *2*, then press Enter.** Page two appears in the window.

12. Choose page 6 from the Page drop-down list.

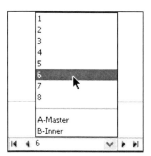

Document Scrolling

You can scroll horizontally and vertically to view each document page. By dragging the scroll frame, you can move quickly to the beginning or end of a document. You can use the Hand tool as an alternate to scrolling. It enables you to move the page by dragging it directly. The Hand tool is convenient, because you can use it to scroll diagonally without having to click in more than one place as you would have to with the scrollbars. You can select the Hand tool in the Toolbox, or can temporarily access it by holding down the Spacebar. You can hold down Alt and drag the page to scroll when you are typing text with the Type tool, since pressing the Spacebar would add spaces to the text.

TASK 1B-3

Scrolling Pages

Objective: To scroll pages.

Setup: The Sample Document.indd file is open.

1. **Click the right scroll arrow as many times as is necessary to see both pages six and seven fully in the window.**

2. **Hold down the mouse button on the down scroll arrow until page eight appears in the window.**

3. **Drag the vertical scroll box to the top of the scrollbar.** Page one appears in the window.

4. **Position the mouse pointer in the middle of the page, then hold down the Spacebar** to access the Hand tool.

5. **Drag the page to approximately center it in the window.**

The Navigator Palette

You can use the Navigator palette, shown in Figure 1-3, to quickly navigate a document. The palette displays the thumbnail of the page to which you most recently navigated, except for scrolling. You can use the slider at the bottom to quickly choose a magnification, or you can use the zoom buttons on the left or right of the slider to change to the nearest preset zoom level. You can also type a zoom percentage in the Magnification field.

Drag the view box within the preview to scroll the document. The part of the document within the view box is the part that displays on screen. Choose View All Spreads from the Navigator palette drop-down list to display thumbnails for all the document pages within the Navigator palette. You can drag from the palette's bottom right to enlarge the palette. Clicking on any page thumbnail within the palette navigates to that page.

You can change the red view box to a different color by choosing Palette Options from the Navigator palette drop-down list.

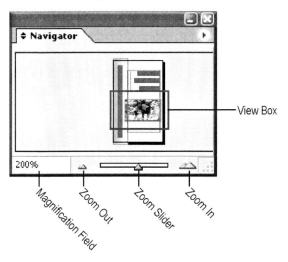

Figure 1-3: *Use the Navigator palette to zoom and scroll a document.*

TASK 1B-4

Navigating with the Navigator Palette

Objective: To navigate a document using the Navigator palette.

Setup: The Sample Document.indd file is open.

1. You'll make the Navigator palette a floating palette so you can move and resize it more easily. **Drag the Navigator palette tab away from the left edge of the screen** where you placed it earlier.

2. You last used the Pages palette to go to the spread of pages six and seven, so they appear in the Navigator palette even though you've scrolled to page one. However, you can change the thumbnail to page one by clicking on something on the page. **Click the Selection tool in the Toolbox.**

3. **Click the picture on page one.** A thumbnail of page one now appears in the Navigator palette.

4. **Position the mouse pointer in the view box inside the Navigator palette.**

5. **Drag the view box in the Navigator palette, then release the mouse button** to move the page within the document window.

6. In the Navigator palette, **click the Zoom In button, which appears as large triangles.** The screen is zoomed to the next preset magnification level.

7. **Drag the Zoom slider in the Navigator palette all the way to the left.** The magnification changes to 5%, in which all of the pages are displayed at a tiny size in the window.

8. **Drag the Zoom slider to the middle.** The magnification returns to approximately 100%.

9. **Choose View All Spreads from the Navigator palette drop-down list.** All of the spreads appear as tiny thumbnails within the palette.

10. **Drag the Navigator palette's bottom-right corner to enlarge the palette.**

11. **Click the spread of pages two and three in the Navigator palette.** Pages two and three appear in the document window.

Navigation Shortcuts

InDesign offers convenient shortcuts for selecting tools, as well as for zooming and scrolling in the document window. Each InDesign tool has a character associated with it that you can type to access it. For example, you can type T to access the Type tool. When you position the mouse pointer on a tool in the Toolbox, a tooltip appears displaying that tool's name and its associated shortcut key. If you're using the Type tool, and the insertion point appears within a frame, then typing any key adds that character to the text frame. In this case, if you want to type a character to select another tool, you must first click in a blank area so that no insertion point appears onscreen. You can then press a key to select another tool.

In addition, you can temporarily access some tools by pressing a particular key or set of keys. This is useful when you're already using a particular tool, and only want to momentarily switch to a different tool, such as for zooming. When you release the key that temporarily accesses a tool, you return to the tool that was selected before you held down the key. For example, you can temporarily access the Zoom tool by holding down Ctrl+Spacebar, and can temporarily access the Zoom Out mouse pointer by holding down Ctrl+Alt+Spacebar. In addition, you can temporarily access the most recently selected selection tool (Selection or Direct Selection) by holding down Ctrl. If you hold down Ctrl and don't get the selection tool you wanted, you can press Tab while still holding down Ctrl to toggle to the other selection tool.

You can also use several keyboard keys to navigate among pages. You can press the Page Up and Page Down keys to view what was just below the window previously. To scroll to the previous or next page, hold down Shift as you press Page Up or Page Down. To scroll to the previous or next spread, hold down Alt as you press Page Up or Page Down.

TASK 1B-5

Using Navigation Shortcuts

Objective: To use shortcuts for navigating through documents, rather than using menus or tools.

Setup: The Sample Document.indd file is open.

1. **Type *T*.** The Type tool is selected. When you are typing text with the Type tool, you can't switch tools with a single-letter shortcut, because that letter would be added to the text.

2. **Zoom out if necessary, and click within the title Head to North Atlantic.**

3. **Type *V*.** The letter v is added to the word.

4. **Choose Edit→Undo Typing.** However, you can click in a blank space to deselect the text, then type another tool's letter.

5. **Click the pasteboard.** No blinking insertion point appears.

6. **Type *V*.** The Selection tool is selected.

7. Since you often need to zoom to specific areas quickly, you can use a shortcut to temporarily access the Zoom tool. **Hold down Ctrl+Spacebar.** The Zoom tool mouse pointer appears.

8. **Click the picture of the students in a laboratory to zoom in.**

9. **Hold down Ctrl+Spacebar+Alt.** The - Zoom mouse pointer appears.

10. **Click the page** to zoom out. When you release those keys, you return to the Selection tool.

11. **Press Page Down twice.**

12. You will now navigate one page at a time. **Hold down Shift and press Page Up twice.**

13. You will now navigate through several spreads. **Hold down Alt and press Page Down twice.**

14. **Choose File→Close.**

15. You will save the changes you made, so you can compare this version of the document to the one you create in the remainder of the course. **Click Yes.** The file closes.

Summary

In this lesson, you've learned the function of InDesign's main tools and window elements, have learned to zoom in and out quickly and easily, and have learned to navigate among pages.

 Lesson Review

1A What is the area outside the pages in the document window called?

What is the difference between the Selection tool and the Direct Selection tool?

1B What keyboard shortcut can you press to access the Zoom tool without using the Toolbox?

List at least two techniques for navigating among InDesign document pages.

Basic Documents

Overview

In this lesson you will create a basic document. You'll create a new InDesign document with the settings you need, and will add formatted text and a placed graphic.

Data Files
Students.jpg

Lesson Time
45 minutes

Objectives

To become familiar with creating new documents, you will:

2A **Set up a new document.**

You will choose the page size, set margins, and choose a number of columns to set up the document's primary layout structure.

2B **Create text on the page.**

You will create text frames, type text, and apply basic formatting. You will resize, move, and rotate text frames both manually and numerically.

2C **Place graphics on the page.**

You will place a graphic created in another application, and will move, resize, and crop it.

 **Topic 2A**

Document Setup

Picas Measurement System

Before you begin setting up your document, you may need to learn about the picas measurement system, which InDesign uses by default. Many designers and typesetters prefer the measurement system of picas and points, since it's the same unit of measurement used for text and images. One pica is 12 points, which is a typical size (height) for a line of body size type.

For example, it is difficult to visualize how many lines of body text will fit vertically beside a graphic when it is measured in inches, because the units do not match. However, it is easy to determine the number of lines that will fit beside a graphic when measured in picas—it will approximately match the height of the image. Approximately four lines of typical body text will fit beside a four pica tall image.

If you are not familiar with the picas and points measurement system, it may take some getting used to. The following conversions will be helpful:

- 72 points=1 inch
- 12 points=1 pica
- 6 picas=1 inch

The notation for picas and points in most applications is [# of picas]p[# of points]. For example, ½ inch is 3 picas or 3p. Likewise, ¾ inch is 4 picas 6 points or 4p6. Also, 6 points can be notated either p6 or 6 pt.

You can enter values in most fields using any supported measurement unit by including a character that specifies the measurement unit. For example, although the default measurement system is picas, you can still enter values in inches by typing the letter i or an inch mark (″) after the value. If you enter a value of 3i in a field, then press Tab, the value appears as 18p, which is the picas equivalent of 3 inches.

When entering a value into a field, you do not have to type the unit if you're using the unit that's set as the current default. When you don't specify a unit of measure, InDesign assumes the default unit (picas by default).

New Document Settings

When you create a new InDesign document, you must first specify the options you want in the New Document dialog box. It is possible to change the document settings later. However, this may be difficult if you have positioned elements on the document's pages. It is best to decide on the correct document settings before you create the document. To create a new document, choose File→New→ Document, then specify settings in the New Document dialog box, shown in Figure 2-1.

In the New Document dialog box, as with other dialog boxes, you can select an existing field value by double-clicking it, allowing you to then type a replacement value. You can then press Tab to move to the next field in the dialog box, or press Shift+Tab to move to the previous field.

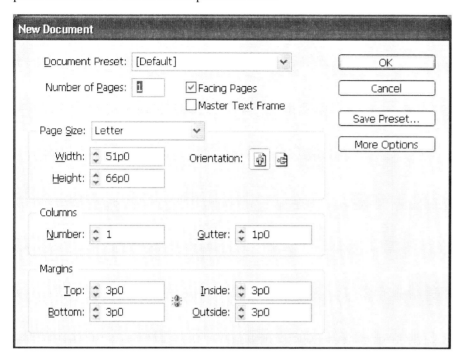

Figure 2-1: *Specify new document settings in the New Document dialog box.*

New Document Setting	Description
Document Preset drop-down list	Contains sets of new document settings you can specify in one step. To create document presets for future use, specify the settings you want in the New Document dialog box, then click Save Preset.
Number Of Pages field	Specifies the number of pages you want the new document to use initially.
Facing Pages check box	Allows you to create a document that contains double-sided pages. Checking this check box provides margin settings of Inside and Outside instead of Left and Right.
Master Text Frame check box	Creates a text frame the size of the space within the document margins on every page. This is useful for text-intensive documents such as books and reports.
Page Size options	Includes the Page Size drop-down list, the Width and Height fields, and the Orientation buttons. From the Page Size drop-down list you can select from several standard page size options. In the Width and Height fields, you can enter values for a custom page size. To set a page size, you can choose from the drop-down list or type your own width and height values in the Width and Height fields. The Orientation buttons allow you to specify a portrait or landscape orientation, controlling whether the width or height is the larger dimension.

If you choose any menu commands with no documents open, the options you set become the new defaults for documents you create from then on. Similarly, if you choose InDesign settings with a document open but no item selected, those settings become the default for new items you create. For example, if you choose a Fill color, shapes you create afterwards in that document will be filled with that color.

You can also create a document preset by choosing File→Document Presets→Define.

New Document Setting	Description
Columns options	Includes the Number field, which specifies the number of columns, and the Gutter field, which specifies the amount of space between columns. The number of columns you specify creates guidelines in the document for the placement of columns; but does not force you to use that number of columns throughout the document. You can even create several text frames on the same page with different numbers of columns. However, it is a good idea to set a number of columns that will match the majority of the document pages.
Margins options	Includes fields that specify the values for each margin. When you specify margins, you are setting the location of the margin guides on the document page. You do not need to place all page elements within these guides; they simply allow you to more easily align objects to a pre-determined margin.

TASK 2A-1

Specifying New Document Settings

Objective: To create a new document with appropriate values in the New Document dialog box.

Setup: InDesign is running with no documents open.

1. **Choose File→New→Document.** The New Document dialog box appears.

2. You want the document to begin with one page, and to use facing pages, 1 column, and no master text frame. All these settings are part of the Default document preset. If necessary, from the Document Preset drop-down list, **select Default.**

3. You will not use the Letter page size. From the Page Size drop-down list, **choose Legal.** The page dimensions are now 51p0 by 84p0.

4. You decide to change the dimensions to a custom size of 8″ x 5″. You'll enter those values using inches. In the Width field, **type 8i.**

5. **Press Tab to select the Height field.** After you pressed Tab, the value of 8i that you entered was converted automatically to 48p0.

6. **Type 5i in the Height field, then press Tab.** The measurement is converted to 30p0. The new measurements are entered. The Page Size menu now shows Custom, since you entered a custom page size. You decide that you want the document to be vertically oriented instead of horizontal.

7. **Click the Portrait icon,** which represents vertical orientation. The numbers for width and height are reversed.

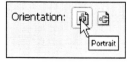

8. You will set each of the margins. You will enter them in picas to familiarize yourself with the system. You want a 1 inch top margin, which is equivalent to 6 picas. **Type *6* in the Top margin field, then press Tab.** You do not have to type p, since the default measurement system is picas.

9. The bottom margin will be 1 inch, like the top margin. **Type *6* in the Bottom margin field, then press Tab.**

10. You will enter the equivalent of 1.5 inches for the inside margin. **Type *9* in the Inside margin field, then press Tab.**

11. The outside margin will be .25 inches. **Type *1p6* in the Outside margin field.**

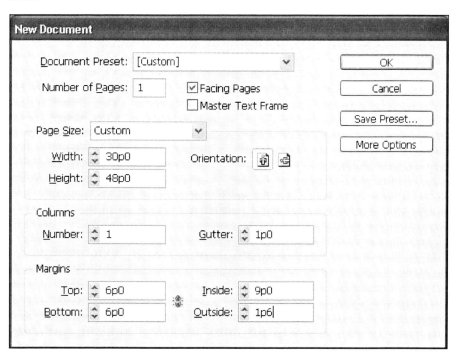

12. Click OK.

13. The new document is created with the title Untitled-1. **Choose File→Save.** The Save As dialog box appears.

14. **In the File Name field, type** *Recruitment Brochure.indd.*

15. **Navigate to the Brochure folder inside the 078195Data folder and click Save.** The document is open for editing, and the margin guides are positioned as you specified in the New Document dialog box.

Topic 2B

Creating Text

The first element you may add to a document is a text frame. Any text in an InDesign document, whether typed directly or imported from a word processing or other file, must be contained in a text frame. To create a text frame, select the Type tool and drag to establish the text frame's dimensions. You can then type to add text within the text frame.

You can resize a text frame at any time after creating it. To resize a text frame, select it using the Selection tool, then drag from one of the corner handles. You can reposition a text frame on the page by dragging from within the text frame using the Selection tool. When you move the frame close to the margins, it is snapped to the guides as if magnetized. The mouse pointer turns white to indicate that the frame is snapped to a guide.

Another way to resize and reposition a page element is to use the Transform palette. The Transform palette allows you to enter dimensions and page location for an element numerically. You can use the Transform palette's proxy to specify the location of any one of nine points on the selected item. Size and position values you specify are then applied to the selected object based on the currently selected proxy point. For example, the Transform palette's X value is the distance from the 0 mark on the horizontal ruler to the point selected in the proxy. The Y value is the distance from the 0 point on the vertical ruler to the point selected in the proxy.

If you wait for a moment while holding the mouse button down before dragging, InDesign's dynamic preview will display the text in the frame as you drag.

When text is too large to fit in a frame, it is considered overset, as indicated by the + symbol that appears at the bottom of the text frame. The + symbol is known as the overset symbol. To alleviate the problem, you could resize the text to fit, enlarge the frame, or thread the current text frame to an empty one.

TASK 2B-1

Creating and Manipulating a Text Frame

Objective: To create a text frame and move it manually and numerically.

Setup: The Recruitment Brochure.indd file is open.

1. You will now create the first text frame on the document. **Click the Type tool** to select it.

2. **Position the mouse pointer anywhere on the page.**

3. **Drag down and to the right to draw a text frame approximately 12 picas (2 inches) wide and 6 picas (1 inch) inch tall.**

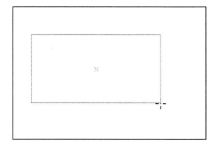

4. The new text frame is created. The text insertion point is flashing inside the frame, indicating that you can now enter text. This frame will contain the title text of the guide. **Type *Where are you headed to school?*** If the text will not fit on one line, the word school wraps to the next line.

5. You will now resize the text frame. **Click the Selection tool in the Toolbox.**

6. If necessary, **click in the text frame.** Selection handles appear around the frame. You will reduce the width of the text frame.

7. **Position the mouse pointer on the lower right corner of the text frame, then drag the corner handle to the left** to reduce the width of the text frame.

8. **Release the mouse button when the text frame is approximately 6 picas (1 inch) tall and 6 picas (1 inch) wide.** The text frame is now resized, and the text has automatically wrapped within the frame.

9. You will move the text frame so it aligns to the top left margin guide. **Position the mouse pointer in the center of the text frame.**

10. **Drag to reposition the text frame so that its upper left corner aligns with the intersection of the top and left margins.**

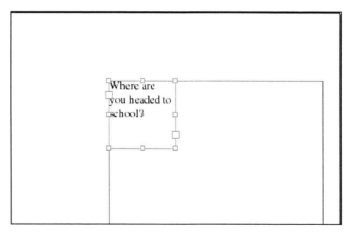

11. You will now reposition and resize the text box using specific values. **Select the text frame if it is not already selected.** For now, you will only change the size and location of the frame.

12. **Choose Window→Transform** to open the Transform palette.

13. You will specify the top-right corner's location. In the Transform palette, **click the top-right corner of the proxy.**

14. **Type *28p6* in the X field, then press Tab.** The right edge of the frame moves to 28p6 across the page, placing it at the right margin. You probably do not need to set the Y location, because you snapped the frame to the top margin guide.

15. If necessary, **type *6p* in the Y field.** You will also resize the frame with the Transform palette.

16. In the W field, **type *18p*.**

17. In the H field, **type** *12p.* You have now set the size and location of the text frame. The rest of the settings do not need to be changed.

18. Press Enter. The text frame is now resized and repositioned on the page.

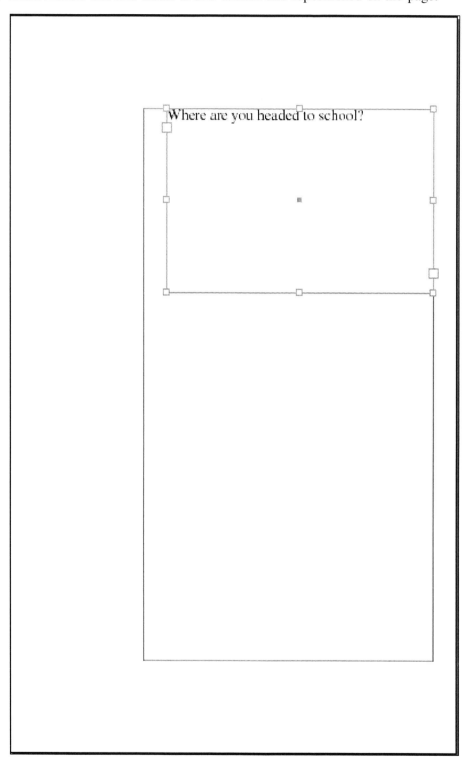

Type Formatting

After you position and size a text frame, you will typically format the text contained in the text frame. If you select a text frame using the Selection tool, any type formatting you choose will apply to all the text within the frame. To format specific text within the frame, select the text using the Type tool. You can select type using the following techniques:

When using the Selection tool, you can double-click a text frame to switch to the Type tool.

- Drag across the text to select it.

- Click twice to select a word.

- Click three times to select a line.

- Click four times to select a paragraph.

- Click five times to select all the text in a text frame or series of threaded text frames. Threaded text frames are a group of text frames that contain a single story that flows from one text frame to another.

You can apply formatting by choosing from the Type menu, Character palette, Paragraph palette, or Control palette. Unlike in many other applications, type styles such as bold and italic are not available as buttons. This is because many fonts were not designed to be boldfaced or italicized, and it would be inappropriate to do so. For example, italicizing a script typeface would make the characters appear to lean too far to the right. Only the type styles appropriate to the specific font are available. This system of selecting fonts allows for fonts with many variations, such as light, medium, book, semibold, bold, and heavy to appear as one font, with variations listed as a submenu to the font, or in the Type Style drop-down list in the Character palette or Control palette.

TASK 2B-2

Formatting Type

Objective: To apply basic formatting to text.

Setup: The Recruitment Brochure.indd file is open.

1. **Select the text frame if it is not already selected.**

The Adobe® Garamond Pro font is located alphabetically in the Font menu by Garamond, not by Adobe®.

2. Choose Type→Font→Adobe® Garamond Pro→Regular.

3. You will change the type to italics, which is available because Adobe® Garamond was designed to include an option for italicizing. In the palette group containing the Transform palette, **click the Character palette tab, and from the Type Style drop-down list, choose Italic.**

4. You will apply boldface formatting to one word. **Select the Type tool in the Toolbox, and select the word "you."**

5. From the Type Style drop-down list, **choose Semibold Italic.** InDesign adds semi-bold formatting to the italic, resulting in Semibold Italic.

6. You will now enlarge the type to nearly fill the frame. **Choose Edit→Select All.**

7. From the Size drop-down list in the Character palette, **choose 36 pt.**

8. You would prefer the type to be slightly larger. You will try the next default type size. From the Size drop-down list in the Character palette, **choose 48 pt.** The text does not all fit in the frame.

9. **Click the Selection tool in the Toolbox and click the frame to select it.** The overset symbol appears in the frame's out port at the bottom right corner when it is selected with the Selection tool.

   In this case, you will resize the text to fit. You will learn about threading text frames in a later section.

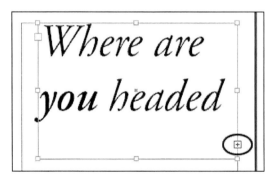

10. Since you need to use a type size that does not appear in the menu, you will enter a size directly using the Character palette. **Click the Character palette tab.**

11. In the Character palette's Size field, **type *44*, then press Enter.** The text is now resized to 44 points, and fits within the frame with the word"you" beginning the second line.

12. Finally, you will right-align the text within the text frame. Horizontal alignment affects the entire paragraph, so you will use the Paragraph palette to right align the text. **Click the Paragraph palette tab.**

13. **Click the Align Right button** .

The text is now right aligned within the text frame.

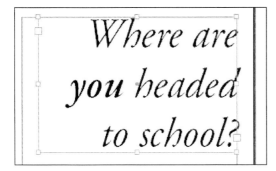

14. **Choose File→Save.**

Vertical Text

In some documents, you may need to create a text frame containing text that flows vertically. You can rotate a text frame by choosing a value from the Transform palette's Rotation Angle drop-down list, or by entering a value into the corresponding field. A positive value indicates a counterclockwise rotation, while a negative value indicates a clockwise rotation.

After rotating a text frame, alignment formatting you apply to the type itself is relative to the text frame's original rotation. For example, you might rotate a text frame 90 degrees counter clockwise. If you then format the text to align right, as shown in Figure 2-2, the text will actually align to the top edge of the text box, which originally was the right edge before rotation.

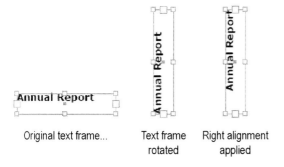

Original text frame...   Text frame   Right alignment
                          rotated   applied

Figure 2-2: *Type alignment is relative to a text box's original rotation.*

You can also align type vertically within a text frame. Vertical alignment is a frame option, not formatting applied to the text within the frame. To vertically align type, choose Object→Text Frame Options. In the Text Frame Options dialog box, choose from the Align drop-down list in the Vertical Justification section.

Since you're likely to use the Text Frame Options dialog box fairly frequently, you might want to remember the shortcut Ctrl+B for accessing it.

TASK 2B-3

Rotating Text

Objective: To create a text frame that is rotated vertically on the page, and to format the text in it.

Setup: The Recruitment Brochure.indd file is open.

1. **Select the Type tool in the Toolbox.**

2. **Position the mouse pointer approximately 6 picas beneath the bottom left corner of the text frame on the page.**

3. **Drag down and to the right to create a text frame approximately 12 picas wide and 6 picas tall.** You can now enter text in the frame with the Type tool.

4. **Type *North Atlantic University* in the text frame.**

5. **Click a blank area on the page.** The insertion point no longer blinks in the text frame. You can now select a tool with a shortcut.

6. **Press V.** You have chosen the Selection tool. You will use it to size and rotate the frame.

7. **Click the text frame you just typed into.**

8. In the Transform palette's H field **type *6*, then press Enter.** The frame is sized to exactly 6 picas tall. You will choose the point about which you want the frame to rotate using the proxy.

9. **Click the top-right proxy point in the Transform palette.** The top-right corner will stay stationary while the rest of the frame rotates.

10. From the Rotation Angle drop-down list, **choose 90°.** The frame rotates 90 degrees counterclockwise about the top-right corner. You can now move the frame into position along the left side of the page.

11. **Drag the selected text frame to the left until its right edge snaps to the left margin.**

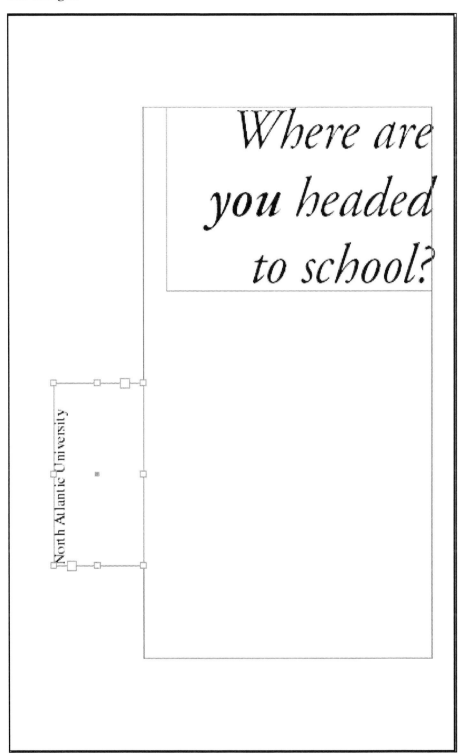

12. You will now enlarge the type to fill most of the left side of the page. **Click the Character palette tab.**

13. **Format the text as Verdana 36 Bold.** The type is now too large to fit in the frame.

14. Drag the top center handle of the frame up until it snaps to the top of the page.

15. Drag the bottom center handle of the frame down until it snaps to the bottom of the page.

16. Drag the left center handle to the left edge of the page.

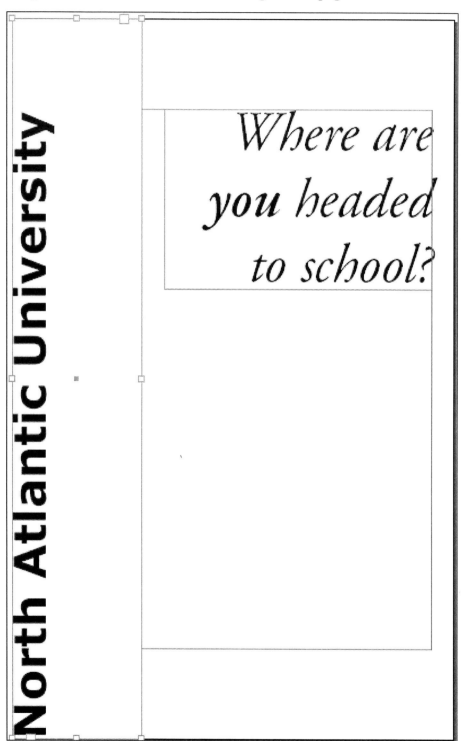

17. You will now center the text within the frame horizontally, relative to the text frame's original orientation. **Click the Paragraph palette tab.**

18. Click the Align Center button. The type is centered, with equal space before and after the characters.

19. You will also align the text vertically. **Choose Object→Text Frame Options.** The Text Frame Options dialog box appears.

20. From the Align drop-down list in the Vertical Justification section, **choose Center.**

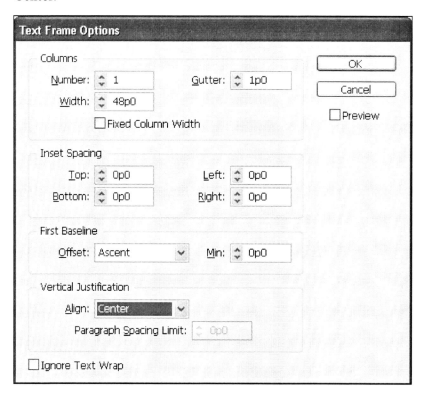

21. Click OK. The type moves to the middle of the frame.

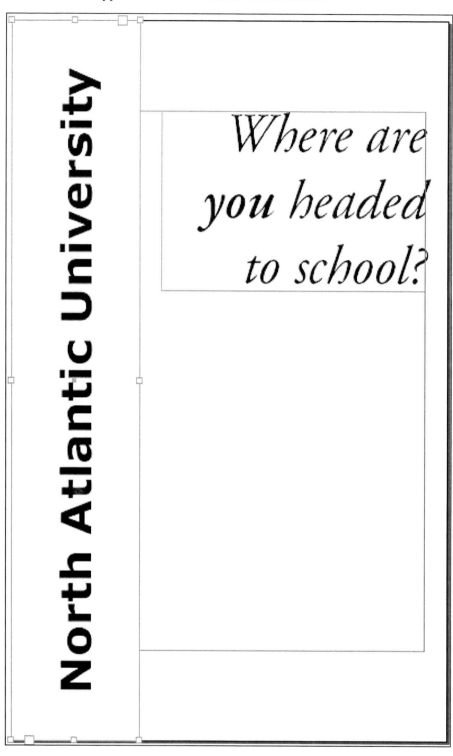

22. Choose File→Save.

Topic 2C

Working with Graphics

Placed Graphics

You've created text frames to contain text. You will now add a frame to contain an imported graphic. You will then use a variety of techniques to resize the graphic.

To import a graphic, choose File→Place, then navigate to and select the graphic you want to place. Click Open, and the mouse pointer then appears as a loaded graphics icon . Click to place the graphic at its original size in the document. Unlike with text frames, InDesign can create frames automatically to fit graphics as they are imported, so you do not need to create the frame first.

Since you're likely to use the Place dialog box fairly frequently, you might want to remember the shortcut Ctrl+D for accessing it.

TASK 2C-1

Placing Graphics

Objective: To place a graphic created in another application.

Setup: The Recruitment Brochure.indd file is open.

1. **Click a blank area of the page.**

2. **Choose File→Place.** The Place dialog box appears.

3. **Navigate to the Brochure folder, and select Students.jpg in the file list.**

4. **Uncheck the Show Import Options check box.**

5. **Click Open.** The mouse pointer appears as a loaded graphic icon .

The Placing Image dialog box may appear briefly with a status bar indicating how much of the image remains to be placed, or a watch mouse pointer may appear.

6. **Position the mouse pointer so the top left corner approximately aligns horizontally with the left side of the Where are you headed to school? text frame and vertically with the top of the letter c in Atlantic.** The Transform palette X and Y values will be approximately 10p6 and 21p3, respectively.

7. **Click to place the image in a new frame on the page.** The picture appears, but is much too large to fit on the page. You will resize the frame next.

Graphic Manipulation

After placing a graphic, you can use the Selection tool to resize the frame containing the graphic so that the frame crops the graphic by hiding the area that does not fit in the frame. To resize the graphic itself, you drag the graphic's corner handles using the Direct Selection tool. You can scale the graphic or the graphic's frame proportionally by holding down Shift as you drag a handle. After scaling the graphic or graphic frame, you must release the mouse button before releasing Shift to ensure that you scale proportionally.

If you want to view the entire graphic, or any selection, so that it fits within the window, right-click the graphic and in the shortcut menu that appears, select Zoom→Fit Selection In Window.

TASK 2C-2

Manipulating Graphics

      Objective: To resize and reposition a placed graphic.

        Setup: The Recruitment Brochure.indd file is open.

1. If necessary, **scroll down and to the right to view the bottom right corner of the image.**

2. You will first resize the graphic frame. **Drag the bottom right corner of the graphic frame up and to the left until the right side of the frame aligns with the right margin and the bottom aligns with the bottom of the letter A in Atlantic.**

3. The image is cropped. You will now move the image within the frame. **Click the Direct Selection tool in the Toolbox.**

4. **Click the picture.** The edges of the original image appear.

5. **Drag the picture up and to the left to approximately center the students in the frame.**

6. To see the picture as you move it, **hold down the mouse button for a few moments before dragging the picture.**

7. The picture is still too large to fit within the frame. You will resize the picture by dragging the picture handles with the Direct Selection tool. Since some of the handles may be outside the window, you will use a shortcut menu to quickly zoom to a magnification that fits the image. **Right-click the picture, then choose Zoom→Fit Selection in Window.** The zoom magnification is changed so you can see all of the picture's handles.

8. **Drag the middle right handle to the left approximately one pica.** Again, if you hold down the mouse button and wait for a moment, InDesign displays a dynamic graphics preview.

9. **Hold down the mouse button for a moment on the middle right handle, then drag it to the left until it approximately aligns with the 33 pica mark on the horizontal ruler.** The image is distorted because you scaled the image horizontally but not vertically. The value in the Scale X Percentage field in the Transform palette is approximately 72%, but the value in the Scale Y Percentage field is still at 100%, so the students now appear too thin. However, you can undo multiple steps, so you can return to the original proportions.

10. **Choose Edit→Undo Resize twice** to return the image to its original size.

11. **Make sure that 100 appears in both the Scale X Percentage and Scale Y Percentage fields in the Transform palette. If necessary, choose Edit→ Undo or Edit→Redo to return to the full size picture.**

12. You will scale the image proportionally. **Hold down Shift, then hold down the mouse button for a moment on the middle right handle, then drag it to the left until it approximately aligns with the 33 pica mark on the horizontal ruler. Release the mouse button, then release Shift.** The picture is scaled proportionally. You can again drag the image within the frame to center the students.

13. Drag the picture to approximately center the students in the frame.

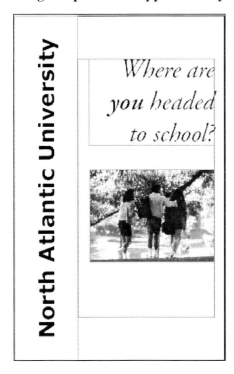

14. The page is complete. You can use InDesign's Preview Mode to view the page as it would appear when printed. **Click the Preview Mode icon at the bottom of the Toolbox.** The guides disappear.

15. The selected graphic frame's handles are still showing. Although you can click a blank part of the page or the pasteboard, there is also a command to deselect all items. **Choose Edit→Deselect All.** The page appears as it would when printed.

16. You should return to Normal View mode to facilitate further editing. **Click the Normal View Mode icon in the Toolbox.** The guides and frame edges reappear.

17. You have now completed the cover for the recruitment brochure. **Save the file.**

Summary

In this lesson you created a basic document using the New Document dialog box and the picas measurement system. You added type into text frames and placed graphics created in other applications. You manipulated the frames and their contents as you moved and rotated them, formatted text, and cropped and resized a picture.

Lesson Review

2A How do you type values in inches when the default measurement system is set to picas?

How can you create a new document and specify its document settings?

2B What do X and Y represent in the Transform palette?

Why are there no buttons for applying type styles such as bold and italic in InDesign?

2C Which tool (Selection tool or Direct Selection tool) do you use to crop an image?

How can you import a graphic into an InDesign document?

Master Pages

Data Files
*Recruitment Brochure.
indd*

Lesson Time
30 minutes

Overview

You should use master pages to structure your document and to make it simpler to work in. Master pages act like backgrounds to document pages, and can be used throughout the document. In this lesson, you'll set up multiple master pages in your InDesign document, add items to masters, apply masters to document pages, and change master items on document pages.

Objectives

To become familiar with master pages, you will:

3A   **Create a new master.**

You'll set up a new master in a fashion similar to setting up a new document, defining margins and columns. You will add additional guides to help place page elements accurately, and will add elements, such as page numbering, lines, and placeholder text, that you wish to repeat on several pages.

3B   **Apply masters to document pages.**

You will choose which master to assign to each document page. You will use different methods of applying masters to individual pages or several at a time. You will convert master items to document items as you replace placeholder text with text you wish to appear on document pages.

Topic 3A

Creating Masters

InDesign offers powerful features for creating and editing multi-page documents. Among these features is the ability to base document pages on master pages. Master pages contain text and images that you wish to repeat on multiple pages in the document. For example, you may want a page number on every page of a document. Instead of creating that page number manually on each document page, you could create it once on the master page. The page number would then appear on every document page. Some common elements that are created on master pages include ruler guides, page numbers, headers, footers, and watermarked (dimmed) text or images.

You may create different master pages for different purposes. For example, the inside pages of a brochure may have different margins than the cover, and should include other elements such as page numbers. Longer documents could have different master pages for different sections, or master pages for section dividers.

A new document initially contains only one master page, labeled A-Master. You can examine and edit master pages by double-clicking them in the Pages palette. To create a new master page, from the Pages palette drop-down list, select New Master. In the New Master dialog box that appears, you can choose a prefix, which will appear on the document page icons in the Pages palette to which you have applied the master. For example, pages based on the default master page A appear with an A in the Pages palette. You can also enter a name for the new master page in the Name field.

In the New Master dialog box, you can base the new master on an existing master by choosing from the Based On Master drop-down list. For example, if all of the masters should have the same image in the same place on the page (for example, a company logo), but differ in other ways, you could base several masters on one that includes the logo. Then, if you repositioned the logo on the main master page, the ones based on it would change as well, while retaining the other differences.

Each master can have different margins and number of columns. To specify margin and column settings for a master, choose Layout→Margins And Columns.

TASK 3A-1

Creating a New Master

Objective: To create a new master, choosing margins and guide settings.

Setup: The Recruitment Brochure.indd file is open.

1. Before adding text and images to the Recruitment Brochure.indd document, you will work on the document's master pages. If necessary, **click the Pages palette tab** to display the palette's contents.

2. **Double-click the words A-Master in the Pages palette.** The master page appears as a spread, because you set this document up as double-sided. This master page is good for the front and back cover, but the margins are not appropriate for the body of the document. You will create another master for that purpose.

3. **Choose New Master from the Pages palette drop-down list.** The New Master dialog box appears. You will call this the Inner master, since you will use it for all inside pages.

4. In the Name field, **type *Inner.***

5. You do not need to base the second master on the original one, since they will be completely different. If necessary, **choose None** from the Based on Master drop-down list.

6. This master should have a left and right page, because the margins should mirror one another. If necessary, **type *2*** in the Number of Pages field. The new master settings are complete.

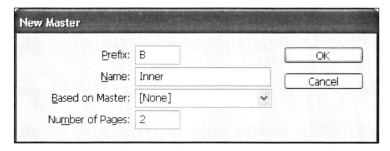

7. **Click OK.** B-Inner appears as a facing pages icon in the Pages palette. You will now change its settings and add elements to it.

8. You wish for the inside of this document to have two columns, with different margins than the current ones. **Choose Layout→Margins and Columns.** The Margins and Columns dialog box appears.

9. In the Top field, **type *4p6.***

10. In the Bottom field, **type *4p6.***

11. In the Inside field, **type *2p3.***

12. In the Outside field, **type *3.***

13. You will use two columns with a 1 pica gap between them (gutter) for the inside of the brochure. In the Number field in the Columns section, **type *2.***

14. If necessary, type *1p0* in the Gutter field. The margins and columns settings are complete.

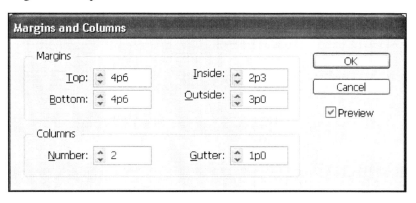

15. Click OK.

Ruler Guides

In addition to the column and margin guides, you can add ruler guides to help you more accurately position text and images on document pages. Like the other guides, ruler guides are non-printing. However, you can place them anywhere on either page, or across both pages. To add a ruler guide, drag from within the horizontal or vertical ruler to place a guide. Dragging a ruler guide onto a page adds the guide only to that page, rather than across both pages in a spread. If you drag a guide and release it on the pasteboard, it will extend across both pages of a spread. After adding a guide, you can continue to drag it to reposition it. To remove a guide, you can drag it back into the ruler, or click the guide to select it, then press Delete.

If you want to lock or unlock the ruler guides, choose View→Lock Guides to check or uncheck it. If you want to hide or show the ruler guides, choose View→ Hide Guides or View→Show Guides.

As you add and move guides, you can view their position numerically using the Transform palette. However, depending on the zoom percentage at which you are viewing the document, it may be difficult to get the guide to the exact measurement you want. It is typically easiest to place guides at even ruler increments when viewing at a percentage that is a multiple of 100. However, you can type the guide location in the Transform palette rather than having to position it manually.

Ruler guides, along with margin guides and column guides, make up the *design grid*. It is a good idea to create a design grid before placing elements on the document to maintain a consistent look from page to page.

Baseline Grid and Document Grid

You can display two kinds of nonprinting grids using the View menu: A *baseline* grid or a document grid. You won't use either in this document, but they can be useful in creating layouts for complex documents. A baseline grid is used for aligning columns of text. For example, if you have two columns of text next to each other, you would want the text in each column to line up with the other columns. Onscreen, a baseline grid resembles notebook paper, as shown in Figure 3-1.

Although it's a good idea to choose View→Lock Guides to prevent the possibility of accidentally moving them when you intend to move something else on the page, you may find that it is difficult to get type to flow into the correct type frame when two frames are snapped to the same locked guide.

design grid:
The combination of margins and guides that helps you structure a document as you design it.

baseline:
The invisible line on which most letters sit.

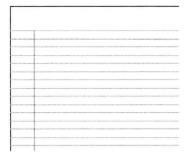

Figure 3-1: *A baseline grid.*

A document grid is useful for aligning objects, and looks like graph paper, as shown in Figure 3-2.

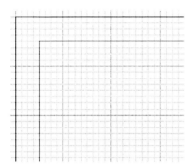

Figure 3-2: *A document grid.*

You can customize both kinds of grids to make the lines closer or farther apart. To add or modify a grid, choose Edit→Preferences→Grids, then specify the color and spacing of the grids. To show or hide the baseline grid, choose View→Show/Hide Baseline Grid. To show or hide the document grid, choose View→Show/Hide Document Grid. You can also choose View→Snap To Document Grid so that objects snap to the grid as you manipulate them.

TASK 3A-2

Creating Ruler Guides

Objective: To create horizontal and vertical guides to help place page items quickly and accurately.

Setup: The Recruitment Brochure.indd file is open.

1. **Position the mouse pointer in the horizontal ruler at the top of the window.**

2. **Drag down onto the left page and release the mouse button.** You have created a horizontal guide. Since you released the mouse button on the left page, the guide only appears on that page, and not on the right one.

3. If necessary, **scroll to view the pasteboard to the left of the master pages.**

4. **Drag the guide you just created on the left page to the left.**

5. **Release the mouse button when the mouse pointer is on the pasteboard.** The guide spans the spread rather than just one page. You will reposition the guide to designate the bottom of the headline frame.

6. **Position the mouse pointer on the guide on the pasteboard.**

7. **Drag the guide up or down so it approximately aligns with the 9p6 mark on the vertical ruler. Release the guide with the mouse pointer on the pasteboard, and view the Transform palette to see the exact location.**

8. You will set the guide's position numerically. If necessary, **click the guide, type *9p6* in the Y field in the Transform palette, and press Enter.** The guide is in position. The guide marks the bottom of the text frame you will place at the top of the page. It will also appear on document pages to allow you to align text and graphic frames below it.

9. You will create another guide that spans both pages and the pasteboard in order to help align rules and a page number frame at the bottom of the page. **Drag a guide from the horizontal ruler to the pasteboard to the left of the master pages.**

10. **Release the mouse button when the guide aligns with the 45p mark on the vertical ruler.**

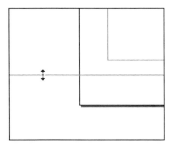

11. If necessary, **click the guide, type *45p* in the Y field in the Transform palette, and press Enter.** The guide spans both pages.

12. You can also create vertical guides. **Drag a guide from the vertical ruler at the left side of the window to the left page until it aligns with the 1 pica mark on the horizontal ruler.**

13. If necessary, **click the guide, type *1p* in the X field in the Transform palette, and press Enter.**

14. Unlike margin guides, ruler guides extend to the top and bottom of the page, which can aid you in positioning elements below the margins but aligned with them. **Drag a guide from the vertical ruler to the left page until it snaps to the outside margin guide at 3p0.**

15. Drag a guide from the vertical ruler to the left page until it snaps to the inside margin guide at 27p9.

16. Drag two guides from the vertical ruler that snap to the inside and outside margins of the right page.

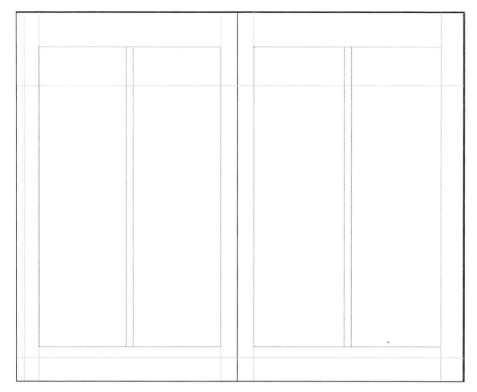

Master Page Text Frames

After specifying master pages, you can create items on those master pages, using guides to align the items. You can often save time, ensure consistency, and make it easier to envision the final design for each page in a layout by creating placeholder frames on master pages. You can add and format placeholder text within the placeholder frame, then replace the placeholder text with the real text on each document page. Adding placeholder text gives you a preview of how the final text will appear formatted. In addition, when you replace the placeholder text with the real text on the individual pages, the formatting you specified is already applied.

Overlapping Text Frames

By default, when one text frame overlaps another, the text in the two frames overlaps as well. You can use the Text Wrap palette to control how text wraps when its frame overlaps another text frame. To open the Text Wrap palette, choose Window→Type & Tables→Text Wrap. The Text Wrap palette's options are shown in Figure 3-3. After specifying a text wrap, you can specify offset values, or the distance from each side that other text must keep away.

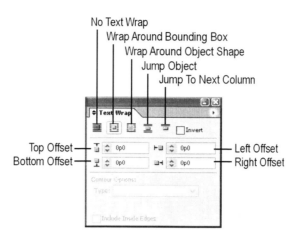

No Text Wrap
Wrap Around Bounding Box
Wrap Around Object Shape
Jump Object
Jump To Next Column

Top Offset —
Bottom Offset —

Left Offset
Right Offset

Figure 3-3: *You can control how text wraps when its frame overlaps another text frame.*

TASK 3A-3

Creating Master Page Text Frames

Objective: To create placeholder text frames, which will allow you to add pre-formatted text to document pages.

Setup: The Recruitment Brochure.indd file is open.

1. Each pair of pages inside the brochure will contain a headline, which you want to span across the spread. You'll create placeholder text frames for the headlines.

    Using the Type tool, **position the crosshair of the I-beam mouse pointer at the intersection of the top and left margins of the left page.** When dragging to create a text frame, the crosshair marks the position of the starting corner.

    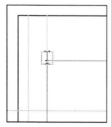

2. **Drag down and to the right to create a text frame that extends to the right margin and down to the guide at 9p6.**

    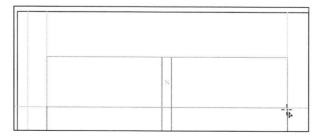

3. You will enlarge this frame to cross the boundary between pages. Using the Selection tool, **click the text frame you just created, then drag the right middle handle to the right column guide of the first column on the right page.** You will also extend the headline to the left of the left margin.

4. **Drag the left middle handle until it snaps to the vertical guide at 1p.**

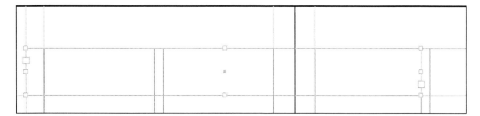

5. The frame will hold a large headline on each pair of pages. **Using the Type tool, click in the frame.**

6. In the frame, **type** *Title Placeholder.*

7. **Format the text as Adobe Garamond Pro 48 point.**

8. Since you will not use the vertical guide at 1 pica on document pages, you can now delete it. **Click a blank part of the page.**

9. Using the Selection tool, **click the vertical guide at 1 pica on the left page.** The guide darkens, indicating that it is selected.

10. **Press Delete.** The guides are now in their final form.

11. You would like the body text on the inside document pages to begin below the headline you created. As it stands now, if you import text, it will flow to the top of the column, overlapping the frame you just created. You must select the frame with the Selection tool to set the text wrap attribute. **Click the text frame you just typed in.**

12. **Choose Window→Type & Tables→Text Wrap.** The Text Wrap palette appears. You will use the second option, which makes text flow either above or below the frame.

13. **Click the Wrap Around Bounding Box icon.**

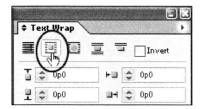

    You wish for body text to begin directly beneath the frame, so you will leave all of the offsets at 0.

14. Body text will be pushed away from the headline frame on the document pages. You no longer need the Text Wrap palette. **Close the Text Wrap palette.**

If you find it inconvenient that guides hide thin lines you create, you can choose Guides & Pasteboard from the Preferences submenu, then check the Guides In Back check box under Guide Options. Page elements will then appear over guides.

The Line Tool

You can draw lines at any angle using the Line tool. In addition, you can hold down Shift while drawing a line to constrain the line to horizontal, vertical, or 45 degrees, depending on the angle at which you drag.

After adding a line, you can format the line's stroke using the Stroke palette. You can use the Stroke palette to specify the line weight, create dashed lines, or add line endings such as arrowheads.

You can duplicate a line, or other InDesign object, by using the Copy and Paste commands in the Edit menu. However, you can copy and paste an object in one step by choosing Edit→Duplicate.

TASK 3A-4

Drawing Lines

Objective: To create lines on the master that will appear on each document page.

Setup: The Recruitment Brochure.indd file is open.

1. You will draw a horizontal line on the left master page using the guide at 45p. In the Toolbox, **select the Line tool**.

2. If necessary, **scroll so you can see the inside, outside, and bottom margins on the left master page.**

3. **Position the mouse pointer at the intersection of the outside margin guide of the left page and the guide you created at 45p.**

4. **Hold down the mouse button and drag to the right until the right endpoint of the line is positioned at the intersection of the inside margin on the left page and the 45p guide.** You have created a horizontal line on the left master page. This line will appear on all left-facing pages that are based on this master page. However, it is difficult to see, because the guide you used is in front of it. You can zoom in to see the line.

5. **Hold down Ctrl+Spacebar and click the line you just created as many times as necessary to increase the magnification to 400%.** The black line is visible along the guide.

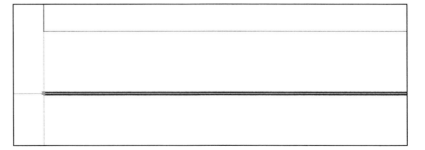

6. Next you will format the line to be thinner. At the screen's bottom right, **select the Stroke tab** to display the Stroke palette.

7. From the Weight drop-down list, **select 0.5 pt.** The line is now very thin.

8. Next you will duplicate the line so you have an identical line on the right page. This is much faster than creating another line and formatting it. **Choose Edit→Duplicate.** You now have a duplicate of the line, which you will move to the right page.

9. **Choose View→Fit Spread In Window.**

10. Using the Selection tool, **click the line to** select it.

11. **Position the mouse pointer on the center portion of the line, then drag the duplicate to the right page.**

12. **Move the line until it snaps to the guide at 45p from the inside margin to the outside margin.** Both left and right pages have a rule at the bottom.

13. **Save the file.**

Page Numbers

Most multiple-page documents include page numbers on each page. Instead of creating page numbers on each page individually, it is much faster and easier to create a page number on the master page. The page number will then appear on every page that is based on that master page. You must first create a text frame to hold the page number. Within the text frame, choose Type→Insert Special Character→Auto Page Number to insert a code that generates the correct page number on each document page.

After formatting the page number code as you want the page numbers to appear, you will typically duplicate the text frame containing the page number to add a copy to the facing page. Instead of using the Duplicate command, you may want to copy and paste the frame so you won't have to drag the duplicate a long distance to position it on the other page. In addition, when copying and pasting a text frame, be sure to select the text frame using the Selection tool so that you copy and paste the entire frame. If you use the Type tool, you copy and paste the selected text in the frame, rather than the entire frame and its contents.

If you want to adjust the position of both text frames at the same time, you should select both text frames by clicking on the first, then holding down Shift and clicking on the second. You can select any two or more items by Shift-clicking. After selecting both text frames, you can press the arrow keys on the keyboard to nudge them in small increments. You can use the arrow keys to nudge any selected items.

You can also insert a page number code by right-clicking within the text frame, and from the shortcut menu that appears, choosing Insert Special Character→Auto Page Number.

TASK 3A-5

Adding Page Numbers

Objective: To create page number codes that automatically appear with the correct page number on document pages.

Setup: The Recruitment Brochure.indd file is open.

1. **Hold down Ctrl+Spacebar and click the line at the bottom of the left page as many times as necessary to increase the magnification to 200%.**

2. **Select the Type tool, then position the mouse pointer at the intersection of the left margin and the guide at 45p.**

3. **Drag down and to the right to create a small text frame that is approximately 6 picas wide and 2 picas tall. Use the Transform palette as a reference as you drag.**

4. You will now enter the page number in this text frame. Instead of typing a number, you will insert a code that will place the correct page number on each page. **Choose Type→Insert Special Character→Auto Page Number.** The letter B appears in the frame, representing a page number placed on master page B. It will be replaced by an actual page number on document pages.

5. Next you will format the contents of this text frame. **Choose Edit→Select All.** The page numbering code is selected.

6. Using the Character palette, **specify Arial Bold, 10 pt.** You will now duplicate the text frame that contains the page number and position it on the right page.

7. **Select the Selection tool.** The frame should be selected, because the text in it was selected when you clicked on the Selection tool.

8. **Choose Edit→Copy.** InDesign copies the text frame and the contents of the text frame.

9. **Scroll to the right to view the bottom of the right page.**

10. **Choose Edit→Paste.**

11. **Drag the duplicate page number frame so its top-right corner lines up with the outside margin and the guide at 45p.**

12. The page number text should be right aligned. In the Paragraph palette, **click the Align Right icon.** Lastly, you should move both page number frames down a bit so the numbers don't touch the lines above them.

13. **Choose View→Fit Spread In Window.**

14. With the Selection tool, **click the page number frame on the left page, then hold down Shift and click the page number frame on the right page.** The two frames are selected. You will nudge them down one point at a time with the arrow keys.

15. Press ↓ six times. The page number code frames move down six points. You have finished adding elements to the master page.

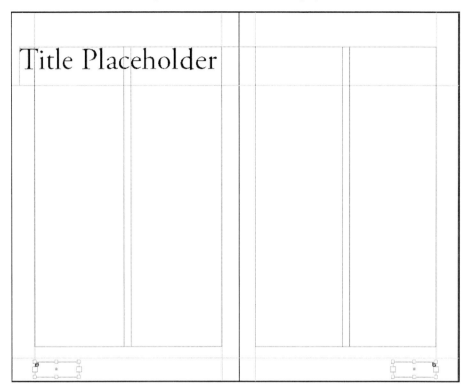

16. Save the file.

Topic 3B

Applying Masters

Once you have created masters, you will apply them to document pages. Each document page is based on one master, and the elements on the master will appear on the document page.

To create a new document page, you can click the New Page button in the Pages palette. By default, new pages are based on the master page used on the previous page. To apply a different master to a document page, in the Pages palette, drag the master's icon or name onto the document page's icon, releasing the mouse button when a dark border appears around the page icon. You can also add a new document page based on a particular master page by dragging the master page icon into the document page section of the palette. In addition, you can create spreads by dragging a master page name to the pages area in the Pages palette. Finally, you can apply a master to multiple document pages at once by first selecting the document pages to which you want to apply the master, then selecting Apply Master To Pages from the Pages palette drop-down list. To select multiple page icons in the Pages palette, Shift-click to select contiguous pages, or Ctrl-click to select discontiguous pages.

TASK 3B-1

Applying Masters to Document Pages

Objective: To create document pages, and to assign a master page to each one.

Setup: The Recruitment Brochure.indd file is open.

1. You will now create document pages, and will apply the B-Inner master to the ones you wish to contain the headline, rules, and page numbering.

   In the Pages palette, **click the New Page button** . A page two appears, using the A-Master master. You will apply the B-Inner master to page two.

2. **Drag the B-Inner master page icon onto the page 2 icon in the Pages palette.**

3. **Release the mouse button when a dark border appears around the page 2 icon.** A B appears on the page 2 icon, indicating that you have applied that master page. The title placeholder, rule, and page number appear on the page in the document window. The number 2 appears for the page number, replacing the code you inserted on the master page. If you create another page after page two, the same master will be applied.

4. **Click the New Page icon in the Pages palette.** A page three is added to the spread with master B applied.

5. You will now add a spread based on the B-Inner master. **Drag the words B-Inner (not the icons next to B-Inner) to the right of the page 3 icon in the Pages palette.** A new spread, containing pages four and five, appears in the Pages palette. .

6. You should now resize the Pages palette to make it large enough to display the icons for all five pages. **Resize the Pages palette until the icons for all five pages are visible.**

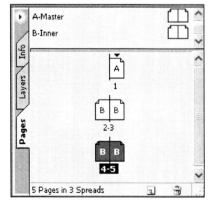

Master Items on Document Pages

After applying masters to document pages, you may want to work with the master page items on the document pages. Master page items ordinarily can't be moved or selected with the Selection tool. However, on a document page, if you hold down Ctrl+Shift and click a master page item, it becomes an editable item on the document page, and is no longer associated with the original master page item. If you wished to return to the original master page, you could delete the item you modified on the document page, then drag the master icon to the page icon in the Pages palette.

TASK 3B-2

Modifying Master Items on Document Pages

Objective: To make changes on document pages to items you originally created on master pages.

Setup: The Recruitment Brochure.indd file is open.

1. **Double-click the page numbers 2-3 in the Pages palette.** The spread of pages two and three appears in the document window.

2. Using the Selection tool, **try to select the frame containing the words Title Placeholder.** The frame cannot be selected. This prevents you from inadvertently making document pages differ from the master they are based on.

3. **Hold down the Ctrl+Shift, then click in the frame containing the words Title Placeholder.** The frame is selected. You can now use the Type tool to change the text.

4. Using the Type tool, **click in the text to establish an insertion point.**

5. **Choose Edit→Select All.**

6. **Type *Head to North Atlantic!* to replace the words Title Placeholder.** You will replace the title on pages four and five as well.

7. **Replace the words Title Placeholder with*Head to Head Action*on page 4.** The titles on the first two inside spreads are complete.

8. **Save and close the file.**

Summary

In this lesson, you created a new master page in addition to the one that was originally in the document. You changed its margins and number of columns, added guides, text frames, lines, and page numbering. You then applied the new master to existing document pages and new pages. Lastly, you replaced placeholder text created on a master with real text on document pages.

Lesson Review

3A What is the main purpose of creating masters?

What is the difference between dragging a horizontal ruler guide to the page or to the pasteboard?

3B How can you type into a text frame that appears on a document page but that was created on a master?

How can you apply a master to a document page using the Pages palette?

Importing and Threading Text

Data Files

Recruitment Brochure. indd
Intro Text.doc
Recruitment Text.doc
Closing Text.doc
History.doc
EOE Text.txt

Lesson Time
30 minutes

Overview

You have created text frames and typed text. You will now import text from a word processing file. After the text appears on the pages, you will modify the way it flows, or threads, from one page to the next.

Objectives

To import and thread text, you will:

4A   Import text.

You'll import text using the Place command.

4B   Thread text throughout the document.

You'll use three methods—manual, semi-automatic, and automatic—to flow, or thread, text from one column to another.

4C   Reflow text threads and change the number of columns.

After importing and flowing text into empty columns, you'll re-flow it into different columns, break and re-establish threads, create multiple column frames, and navigate through threaded text efficiently.

Topic 4A

Importing Text

You can place text regardless of which tool is selected when you choose the Place command.

After setting up pages in a new document, you will often then import the text for the document. As with placing graphics, you do not need to create a frame ahead of time if you are placing text, although you can import text into an existing frame. To place text, choose File→Place, then select the file you want to place and click Open. If you check the Show Import Options check box before selecting your file and clicking Open, then an Import Options dialog box will appear, with settings specific to the type of file you're importing. These settings allow you to control some formatting and other attributes of the text as you import it. For example, when you import text or tables from Microsoft Word or Excel files, you can specify that the contents import as unformatted text. In addition, for most types of files, you can specify that quote marks import as typographer's quotes (as opposed to tick marks).

InDesign can read the text and formatting from several file formats, including Microsoft Word, WordPerfect, Microsoft Excel, and any ASCII text or Rich Text Format (RTF) file. Although some formatting, such as margins and borders around paragraphs, is ignored, InDesign uses import filters to translate the majority of the formatting.

After importing text, the mouse pointer turns into a loaded text icon [icon], allowing you to click to specify where you want the text to be placed. If you click at a column guide, InDesign will automatically flow the text into that column.

InDesign Stories

An InDesign story is one continuous body of text. The text in a story can be flowed into one frame, or spread across several threaded frames. The text frames do not have to be adjacent. For example, you can continue a story from page one onto page ten. To add more text to an existing story, you must position the insertion point where you want the additional text to be inserted before you type or place text.

TASK 4A-1

Importing Text from Files

Objective: To import text throughout the document.

Setup: The Recruitment Brochure.indd file is open.

1. You will place text beginning on page two. From the Pages drop-down list, **choose 2.**

2. With the Selection tool, **click a blank area on the page to deselect all frames.** You can now place text into a new frame.

3. **Choose File→Place.** The Place dialog box appears.

4. You will import the document Intro Text.doc, which is a Microsoft Word for Windows file. **Click Intro Text.doc once in the file list** to select it.

5. **Check the Show Import Options check box, then click Open.** The Microsoft Word Import Options dialog box appears.

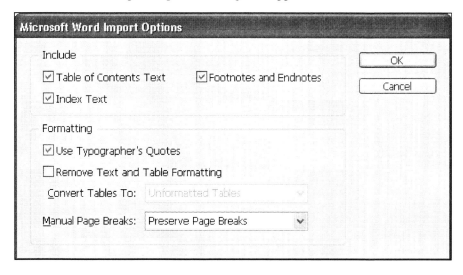

6. You will use the default settings. **Click OK.**

7. The mouse pointer appears as a loaded text icon 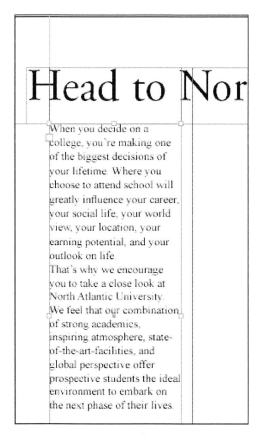. **Position the mouse pointer at the intersection of the left margin guide and the ruler guide at 9p6 on page two (the left page).**

8. **Click to flow the text into the first column.** InDesign imports the text and the text flows into the first column.

9. You will now import more text into this story. Using the Type tool, **click beneath the text in the first column.** The insertion point appears on the line after the text.

10. You can place more text to add to the story. **Choose File→Place.** The Place dialog box appears.

11. **Select Recruitment Text.doc, and uncheck the Show Import Options check box.** This is also a Microsoft Word file.

12. **Check the Replace Selected Item check box, then click Open.** InDesign imports the text and flows it into the left column. This word processor document was formatted differently than the prior one; however, you will reformat all of the text in the story at once later.

13. The document you placed is too long to fit in the column, so an overflow symbol appears at the bottom right corner of the text frame. You will continue to flow the text onto the document pages in the next topic. **Save the file.**

Topic 4B

Threading Text

InDesign offers a few ways to continue text from one column to another or one page to another. This process is called threading text frames. You can flow text manually, semi-automatically, or automatically, depending on whether you need to control the placement of the text you are flowing or not.

You can flow text into or out of any text frame by using the in and out ports. In ports are the small boxes at the top left and out ports are the small boxes at the bottom right. Symbols in the ports indicate the frame's status, as shown in Figure 4-1. An empty in port represents the beginning of a story; an empty out port indicates that the frame is the last one in a story. An arrow in an in port indicates that text is continued from another frame; an arrow in an out port indicates that it continues from this frame to another. Lastly, the +, or overset symbol, indicates that there is unseen text that exists beyond what is in the frame, but the frame is not threaded to another one.

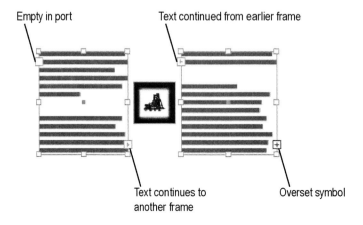

Figure 4-1: *Symbols in the ports indicate the frame's status.*

Manual Text Threading

When you wish to continue text from one frame to another, you essentially connect its out port to the other frame's in port. One technique is to use the Selection tool to click the first frame's out port. The mouse pointer then appears as a loaded text icon. You can then designate another frame or location into which to flow the remaining text. If you click an existing frame, the remaining text from the first frame will flow into that frame, pushing any pre-existing text to the end of the story. If you click in an empty column, InDesign will create a new frame that is the width of the column and that extends to the bottom. When you position the loaded text mouse pointer within an existing frame, it appears as a chain icon. When you position the loaded text mouse pointer close to guides, it appears as a white arrow, indicating that the generated text frame will snap to the dimensions of the column guides.

TASK 4B-1

Threading Text Manually

Objective: To thread text from one column into another.

Setup: The Recruitment Brochure.indd file is open.

1.   You will begin by threading this text to the second column on page two. Using the Selection tool, **click the red + in the first column's out port at the bottom right corner of the frame.** The mouse pointer becomes a loaded text icon. You will flow the text to the second column.

2.   **Position the mouse pointer in the second column on page 2 so the top left corner is at the intersection of the column guide at the right side of the gutter and the ruler guide at 9p6.**

3.   If you position the mouse pointer in the headline frame above the column, the mouse pointer displays a chain, indicating that you would be threading the text into an existing frame. You want to ensure that the text will flow into a new frame that will snap to nearby guides. **Make sure the small arrow at the top left corner of the loaded text icon appears white by moving it close to the guides.**

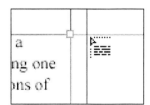

4.   **Click to place the text in the second column.**

5.   If the text flows anywhere other than into the second column, **choose Edit→ Undo, move the mouse pointer slightly, and try again.** The text continues into the second column.

6.   If necessary, **drag the top center handle up so it snaps to the horizontal guide at 9p6.**

Semi-Automatic Text Flow

When you flow text from one frame to another, it ordinarily stops at the new frame, and an overset symbol appears in the new frame if the text doesn't all fit. If you wish to continue flowing the text, you must click the overset symbol again. However, if you hold down Alt when you click to flow text from one frame to another, the mouse pointer automatically appears again as a loaded text icon if there's additional overset text in the new frame.

TASK 4B-2

Flowing Text Semi-Automatically

Objective: To automatically get a loaded text icon after flowing text so you can continue flowing it.

Setup: The Recruitment Brochure.indd file is open.

1. You will use the semi-automatic text flow technique to place text in the columns on page three.**Click the overset symbol in the out port of the second column's text frame.** The loaded text mouse pointer appears again.

2. **Position the top left corner of the mouse pointer at the intersection of the left margin guide and the ruler guide at 9p6 on page three.**

3. **Hold down Alt.** The mouse pointer changes to one with a dotted curving line, indicating that InDesign will load the mouse pointer again after you place text in the next frame.

4. While still holding down Alt, **click to place the text in the column.** The text flows into the left column on page three.

5. If the text flows anywhere other than into the left column, **choose Edit→ Undo, move the mouse pointer slightly, and try again.** However, unlike the last time you flowed the text, the mouse pointer remains a loaded text icon, so you can continue to flow the text elsewhere.

6. If necessary, **drag the top center handle up so it snaps to the horizontal guide at 9p6.**

Automatic Text Flow

If you hold down Shift as you click with a loaded text icon to continue text in a new frame, the text will automatically flow into as many additional frames as necessary to display all the text.

TASK 4B-3

Flowing Text Automatically

Objective: To flow text automatically into the next available columns.

Setup: The Recruitment Brochure.indd file is open.

1. You wish to continue to flow the remainder of the text into the next available columns. **Position the top left corner of the mouse pointer at the top left corner of the right column on page three. Make sure you are at the top of the column, and not at the ruler guide at 9p6.**

2. **Hold down Shift.** The mouse pointer changes to one with a solid curving line, indicating that after the column you create now, it will continue to flow the text into columns as necessary.

3. While still holding down Shift, **click to place the text in the column.** The text flows into the right column of page three, and continues on page four.

4. **Double-click the page numbers 4-5 in the Pages palette.** The text ends in the right column of page four.

5. **Click the frame in the right side of page four.** The frames on page four start at the top of the page, rather than at the ruler guide at 9p6. However, the text does not begin until 9p6, because you applied a text wrap to the headline frame on the B-Inner master. The body text in the two column frames is forced to begin outside the headline frame.

   The in port of the right column frame contains a triangle, indicating that text is flowing into the frame from elsewhere, but the out port is empty, indicating that this is the last frame in the story.

6. **Save the file.**

Topic 4C

Changing Text Threads

Now that you have learned to thread text manually, semi-automatically, and automatically, you will learn further techniques to thread text. You will thread text into multiple column frames, unthread text, let InDesign create pages automatically when automatically flowing text, delete threaded frames, insert frames into existing text flows, view text threads, and navigate through threaded text frames.

Threads to Existing Frames

When you want to thread text into an existing frame, you position the loaded text icon within the existing frame. The mouse pointer will appear as a chain link icon, indicating that the text will be threaded to the existing frame rather than to a new frame.

TASK 4C-1

Threading to Existing Frames

Objective: To thread text into frames that already exist rather than creating frames automatically with the loaded text mouse pointer.

Setup: The Recruitment Brochure.indd file is open.

1. You will create a text frame on page five to experiment with threading text into existing frames. Using the Type tool, **position the crosshair of the I-beam mouse pointer at the intersection of the left margin guide and the ruler guide at 9p6 on page five.**

2. You must position the mouse pointer a bit away from the existing headline frame to avoid clicking in it. If necessary, **move the mouse pointer down and to the right slightly to make sure the I-beam mouse pointer has a dotted frame around it.**

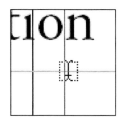

3. **Drag down and to the right to the bottom right corner of the column.** The frame is created. If you were close enough to the guides, the frame edges snapped to them.

4. If necessary, **access the Selection tool temporarily, click in the frame you just created, and drag the top left corner up to the intersection of the left margin and the ruler guide at 9p6, then return to the Type tool.**

5. You will place more text into the story you started, and will flow the text from the previous page into the new frame. **Click at the bottom of the frame in the right column of page four.** An insertion point appears at the end of the last line of text.

6. You will add a line before placing additional text. **Press Enter.** The insertion point moves to the blank line following the text, which may not fit in this text frame.

7. **Choose File→Place, then select Closing Text.doc, and click Open.** The overset symbol indicates that it will not fit in the frame.

8. You will flow the text into the empty frame on page five manually so you can experiment with this one frame, rather than create all of the remaining ones automatically. Using the Selection tool, **click the overset symbol in the out port of the frame in the right column of page four.**

9. **Position the mouse pointer anywhere within the empty frame in the left column of page five, then click to flow the text into the frame.** The text appears in the frame, and the overset symbol appears, indicating that there is more text than fits in the frame.

Multiple Column Text Frames

As an alternative to flowing text into one frame per column, you can create frames that hold multiple columns. Flowing text into a multiple column frame makes it easier to manipulate two or more columns at once, and can allow you to experiment more freely with column widths and number of columns. With a multiple column frame, you cannot inadvertently change the gutter by dragging one column.

To adjust the number of columns within a frame, select the frame, then choose Object→Text Frame Options. In the Text Frame Options dialog box, in the Columns section, enter the number of columns you want within the Number field. The Width field in the Columns section represents the width of each column, not the width of the entire frame. Therefore, if you knew the column width and gutter you wanted, you could enter them directly, and InDesign would calculate the total frame width. If you later manually change the width of the frame, the column widths will change as well.

An alternate option is to fix the column width, so that dragging the text frame width creates or removes columns instead of widening or narrowing the existing ones. To do so, choose Object→Text Frame Options, and check the Fixed Column Width check box. Now if you widen the frame, InDesign will create additional columns, because the column width is not allowed to change.

TASK 4C-2

Formatting Text Frames with Multiple Columns

    Objective: To create and format a text frame that holds multiple columns of text.

    Setup: The Recruitment Brochure.indd file is open.

1. You will change the frame on page five to two columns to experiment with multiple-column text frames. You will first widen the frame to span both columns. **Drag the right middle handle to the right margin on page five.** The text is still in one column, but the column is widened.

2. You will now specify options for the text frame. **Choose Object→Text Frame Options.** The Text Frame Options dialog box appears.

3. **Click the up arrow icon to the left of the Number field to change the value to 2.** The Width value decreased automatically when you added a second column, because it represents the width of each column, not the width of the entire frame.

4. You will leave all of the other values at their defaults; you will experiment with some later. **Click OK.** The text now flows in two columns in the frame. The column guides match the gutter of the page guides.

5. **Drag the right middle handle slightly past the right page edge.** The columns widen, and the column guides belonging to the frame are now visible to the right of the page column guides.

6. You will return the frame to its original width. **Drag the right middle handle back to snap to the right margin guide.**

7. You will now adjust settings so that dragging the text frame width creates or removes columns instead of widening or narrowing the existing ones. **Choose Object→Text Frame Options.** The Text Frame Options dialog box appears.

8. **Check the Fixed Column Width check box, then click OK.**

9. **Drag the right middle handle slightly to the right and release the mouse button.** A third column appears, with a 1 pica gutter between it and the second column.

10. If necessary, **scroll to the right to view the right edge of the three column frame.**

11. **Drag the right middle handle slightly to the right again.** A fourth column and third gutter are created.

12. You will experiment with returning the frame to one column. **Drag the right middle handle to the middle of the first column.** The frame becomes one column, because two columns would not fit in the space you designated by dragging.

13. You will return the frame to two columns. **Drag the right middle handle slightly to the right.** The frame snaps to two columns that match the page guides. As you can see, the Fixed Column Width option can help you experiment with layouts. You will leave this frame at two columns.

Frame Unthreading

You may need to unthread text frames that you threaded earlier. You can break the thread from any frame using the same steps you use to manually thread frames. To break the thread from a frame, select the frame that you no longer want to thread to the following frame. Click the triangle symbol in the out port of the selected frame, then position the mouse pointer within the following threaded frame. The mouse pointer appears as a broken link. Click to break the thread.

TASK 4C-3

Unthreading Frames

Objective: To break existing threads, so you can flow text to a different place in the document.

Setup: The Recruitment Brochure.indd file is open.

1. You will break the thread to the two-column frame on page five. **Click the right column of text on page four (the left page).**

2. **Click the triangle symbol in the out port of the selected frame.**

3. **Position the mouse pointer anywhere within the two-column frame on page five.** The mouse pointer becomes a broken link, indicating that clicking would break the thread to this frame.

4. **Click within the two-column frame to break the thread.** The right column frame on page four is now overset.

Automatic Text Threading

When you thread text using the automatic text flow option, InDesign will create additional pages and frames as necessary to contain all of the text. However, you cannot autoflow text into an existing frame.

TASK 4C-4

Creating Pages with Automatic Threading

Objective: To create pages automatically as you thread pages with the automatic method.

Setup: The Recruitment Brochure.indd file is open.

1. You will re-thread to the two-column frame on page five, but this time you will use the automatic text flow option. You will first delete the empty two-column frame you created on page five. **Click the two-column frame on page five, and press Delete.**

2. You can now autoflow text onto page five. **Click the right column of text on page four (the left page).**

3. **Click the overset symbol in the out port of the selected frame.**

4. **Position the top left corner of the mouse pointer at the intersection of the left margin guide and the ruler guide at 9p6 on page five.**

If no page six is added, add it now, so that it uses the B-Inner master page.

5. **Hold down Shift, then click to place the text in the column.** The text flows into both columns on page five, and a page six is created to hold any additional text.

6. **Double-click the page 6 icon in the Pages palette.** The body text that was automatically flowed starts at the top of the column, overlapping the headline text frame. This is because text wrap settings applied to the frames on master pages do not take effect on document pages.

   However, as soon as you convert the headline frame to a document page frame and type, the text wrap will take effect. You will type the correct headline for this spread.

7. **Hold down Ctrl+Shift, then click the title placeholder above the right column.** The frame is converted from a master page frame to a document frame, and the text wrap takes effect. The body text is pushed beneath the headline. You can now type the title.

8. **Change the Title Placeholder to** *Heading for Success...*

Threaded Frame Removal

At times, you may wish to delete a frame from the middle of a series of a threaded story. You can delete a threaded frame by selecting the frame using the Selection tool and pressing Delete. The text that flowed into the frame you removed will be flowed into the following frame in the thread.

TASK 4C-5

Deleting Threaded Frames

      Objective: To delete frames that are in a series of threaded text boxes.

      Setup: The Recruitment Brochure.indd file is open.

1. In this brochure, you want to rearrange your layout to allow for a separate sidebar story in a colored frame to appear in the right column of page three. Therefore, you must make room for that new text by eliminating the column that is currently there. **Double-click the page numbers 2-3 in the Pages palette.** The spread of pages two and three appears.

2. **Take note of the words at the top of the right column on page three.** These words will be flowed to page four when you delete the frame in the right column.

3. Using the Selection tool, **click the right column of text on page three.**

4. **Press Delete.** The column disappears.

5. You will verify that the text flowed directly to page four. **Double-click the page numbers 4-5 in the Pages palette.** The text that was previously in the right column of page three is now on page four.

6. **Save the file.**

Additional Frames in a Series

You may wish to add a frame to the middle of a sequence of threaded frames. Adding a threaded frame between previously threaded ones is much like flowing text from an overset frame, but you click the out port of a frame that is already threaded instead of the last one in the series.

In addition, you may want to thread the last frame in a series to an empty frame to allow for the text to flow if it later becomes overset due to formatting changes, the addition of graphics among the text, and other layout changes. To specify an empty frame in which a story can flow as necessary, click the out port of the final frame in a story. Even though the out port appears empty, a loaded text icon appears so you can designate where you wish for the text to flow next. You can then click elsewhere to create an empty frame threaded to the previous frame.

Loaded Text Icon Control

If you ever place text, then select the Undo command, a loaded text icon appears so you can re-place the text. You can then place the text elsewhere, or choose to cancel placing the text altogether. If you ever wish to cancel placing text when you have a loaded text icon, you can simply click another tool in the Toolbox. For example, this technique can be useful when you accidentally click a text frame's out port.

You can perform many operations, such as switching pages and creating new pages, even while you have a loaded text icon mouse pointer.

TASK 4C-6

Inserting Frames in a Series and Canceling Text Flow

> **Objective:** To add a frame to the middle of a series of threaded ones and to cancel text flow that you have begun.
>
> **Setup:** The Recruitment Brochure.indd file is open.

1. **Double-click the page 3 icon in the Pages palette.** Page three appears in the window.

2. **Click the left column of text on page three.**

3. **Click the triangle in the out port of the left column of text on page three.** The mouse pointer turns into a loaded text icon.

4. You will now place the text into the empty right column. **Position the top left corner of the mouse pointer at the top left corner of the right column on page three.** Make sure you are at the top of the column, and not at the ruler guide at 9p6.

5. **Click to place the text.** A new threaded frame is inserted in the right column of page three.

6. You reconsider, and decide that you do want to vacate the right column to allow for a sidebar story. In this case, you can simply undo the last action. **Choose Edit→Undo Place.** The loaded text icon reappears.

7. **Click the Selection tool in the Toolbox.** The loaded text icon disappears.

Text Thread Navigation

When a document contains multiple stories that each flow among multiple threaded frames, it can be useful to display a visual cue as to which frames are threaded to one another. Choose View→Show Text Threads to display lines that connect the out ports of frames to the in ports of the following ones.

You can also use shortcuts to navigate among threaded text frames. Select a threaded text frame, then use one of the following shortcuts to navigate to other frames in the story.

Navigation Shortcut	Action
Ctrl+Alt+Page Down	Navigates to the next frame in the thread.
Ctrl+Alt+Page Up	Navigates to the previous frame in the thread
Ctrl+Alt+Shift+Page Up	Navigates to the first frame in the story.
Ctrl+Alt+Shift+Page Down	Navigates to the last frame in the story.

TASK 4C-7

Viewing and Navigating Through Text Threads

Objective: To verify the threading order of frames, and to move through threaded text efficiently without having to scroll extensively.

Setup: The Recruitment Brochure.indd file is open.

1. **Click the left column of text on page three.**

2. **Choose View→Show Text Threads.** Lines appear from the out ports of frames to the in ports of the following ones.

3. **Scroll down and to the left to view the text thread between pages three and four.**

4. You will view the last frame in the story. **Press Ctrl+Alt+Shift+Page Down.** You are now viewing the last frame of the story on page six. It is overset, because you deleted a frame on page three that got flowed into later frames.

5. You will flow this text into the remaining column to complete the story. **Click the overset symbol in the out port of the frame in the left column of page six.**

6. **Position the top left corner of the loaded text mouse pointer at the intersection of the left edge of the second column and the ruler guide at 9p6.**

7. **Click to place the text in the right column.** The text fits in this column. However, you can anticipate that after formatting and adding pictures, the text will need to occupy more space than it currently does, and will flow onto a new page. You will add a seventh page to the brochure.

8. From the Pages palette drop-down list, **choose Insert Pages.** The Insert Pages dialog box appears. You will add one new page, using the B-Inner master page.

9. **Click OK.** Page 7 now appears, using the B-Inner master page.

10. You will thread to an empty frame on page seven to prepare for future expansion of the text. **Click in the out port of the frame in the right column of page six.** A loaded text mouse pointer appears.

11. **Position the top left corner of the mouse pointer at the intersection of the left margin and the ruler guide at 9p6 on page seven.**

12. **Click to create a new threaded text frame.** You can see by the thread lines that if the text were to overflow page six, it would flow into this new frame on page seven.

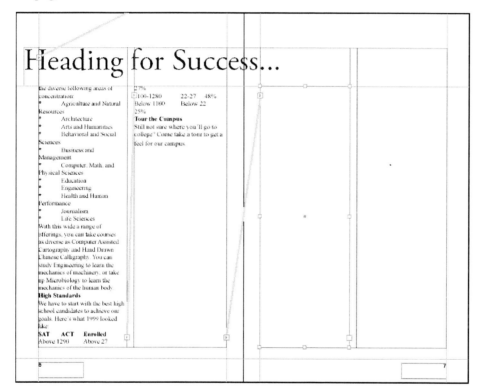

13. You no longer need to see the text threads, since they can be distracting. **Choose View→Hide Text Threads.** The text is flowed correctly.

14. **Save the file.**

Apply Your Knowledge 4-1

Creating and Manipulating Text Frames

You'll now practice what you have learned by navigating in the document as you create and manipulate text frames. You will start a new story in the right column of page three, and will thread it to a frame on another page.

1. Go to page three.

2. Place the file History.doc into the right column of page three. Be sure to start the frame at the top of the column, not at the ruler guide at 9p6.

3. Thread the text into the right column of page seven. Again, be sure to start the frame at the top of the column, not at the ruler guide at 9p6.

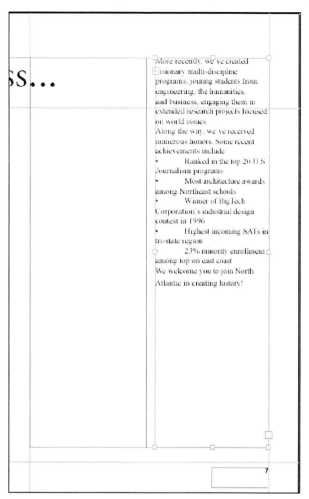

4. You will also create an additional page to act as a back cover, and will add text to it. Insert one additional page after page 7 based on the A-Master page.

5. Create a 15p square text frame on page eight.

6. Import the text file EOE Text.txt into the text frame.

7. Drag the text frame so the bottom edge snaps to the bottom margin.

8. Change the type to Arial 9 point, centered.

9. Drag a vertical ruler guide to the 15 pica mark on the horizontal ruler on page eight.

10. Align the center handles of the type frame to the guide at 15 picas to visually center the frame on the page.

11. Save and close the document.

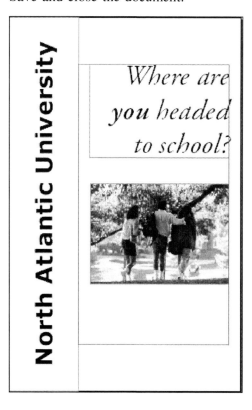

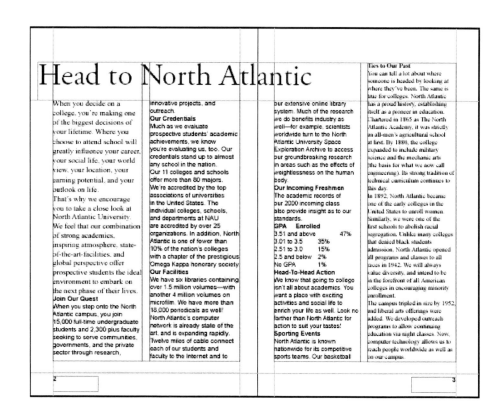

Head to Head Action

team is perennially a top contender in our conference, and our women's lacrosse team competes on a national level for top ranking. And, of course, you won't want to forget to pick up your tickets to see North Atlantic's football team in a bowl game each year.

But it's not just the big name sports that we excel in. North Atlantic offers volleyball, track and field, golf, and many other sports. You can try out for one of our intercollegiate teams, or just play a pickup game of basketball or frisbee on one of the many recreation fields interspersed throughout the campus. Either way, you'll find North Atlantic to be ripe with athletic opportunities.

Fraternities & Sororities

Want other ways to get involved? The dozen Fraternity and Sorority chapters at North Atlantic provide a great way to connect with other students as well as the surrounding community. Many of our pledges develop as leaders through community service and planning social activities.

Culture

North Atlantic is proud to be a cultural center for our region. Attend one of the critically acclaimed theatrical productions in the 1,100-seat Freeman Theatre. Or, enjoy exhibitions at the Matthews Art Gallery, highlighting the work of many students in our esteemed school of art. For musical enjoyment, come to events as diverse as a string quartet recital or a rehearsal of the North Atlantic Marching Band.

North Atlantic Student Center

Our Student Center is a great place to meet a friend, grab a bite to eat, or catch a movie. It's home to a Cilantro's Mexican restaurant, along with university eateries, our giant bookstore, and a video arcade.

Action Off Campus

At North Atlantic, you can build adventure into your academic program as well. We strongly encourage all of our students to head out of the classroom and into the world. We'll point you to one or more of the thousands of opportunities for internships in locations throughout the Northeast. We have students assisting on newspaper staffs in major cities, helping environmental groups to clean up the Vermont woodlands, and designing composite materials for companies such as Badweather Umbrella Corporation.

The Surrounding Region

One of the best aspects of coming to North Atlantic is breathing in the crisp Vermont air and enjoying its natural beauty. You don't have to stray far from the campus to find scenic mountains with deep snow, pristine lakes, and babbling streams. Visitors from around the globe come to witness our spectacular views. Vermont is graced with 15 alpine ski areas and 47 cross country centers, as well as more than 2000 miles of marked and groomed snowmobile trails, so you can get your exercise in the great outdoors as well.

We also encourage students to make their way downtown to explore local culture. Greenville's own Maple Syrup Farm and the nearby Centre City Symphony are great places to begin your journey into the

Northern New England lifestyle

We take great measures to ensure that each North Atlantic student's experience is a success story. Our curriculum and faculty will help get you where you want to go in life.

Research Opportunities

NAU is a public research university. What that means to you is that the author of your textbook may be teaching you directly. Our faculty doesn't just teach - they do. They create new technologies, initiate medical breakthroughs, discover ways to improve the environment. Whatever your major, North Atlantic faculty has experts on board to take your knowledge and experience farther than you can imagine.

Be a Big Fish

Unlike at many large schools, you won't get lost in the mix at North Atlantic. We're a big school with a small-school atmosphere. We keep the student to faculty ratio below 10:1 so you can get individualized attention. 3-4 of our undergraduate courses have 35 or fewer students. Two thirds have fewer than 20, so you'll feel like you're attending a much smaller school - while reaping the benefits of attending a well-funded research university.

Career Choices

Opportunities abound for North Atlantic graduates. Choose from

4

6

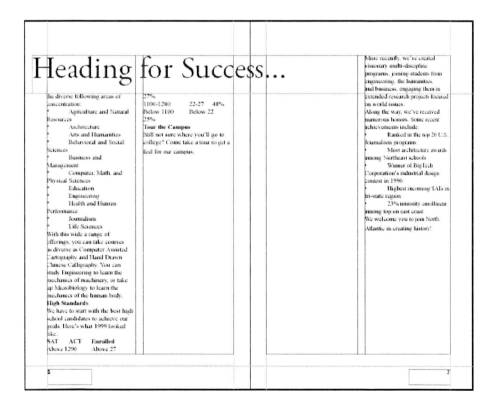

Heading for Success...

the diverse following areas of concentration:
* Agriculture and Natural Resources
* Architecture
* Arts and Humanities
* Behavioral and Social Sciences
* Business and Management
* Computer, Math, and Physical Sciences
* Education
* Engineering
* Health and Human Performance
* Journalism
* Life Sciences

With this wide a range of offerings, you can take courses as diverse as Computer Assisted Cartography and Hand Drawn Chinese Calligraphy. You can study Engineering to learn the mechanics of machinery, or take up Microbiology to learn the mechanics of the human body.

High Standards

We have to start with the best high school candidates to achieve our goals. Here's what 1999 looked like:

SAT	ACT	Enrolled
Above 1290	Above 27	27%
1100-1280	22-27	48%
Below 1100	Below 22	25%

Tour the Campus

Still not sure where you'll go to college? Come take a tour to get a feel for our campus.

More recently, we've created visionary multi-discipline programs, joining students from engineering, the humanities, and business, engaging them in extended research projects focused on world issues.

Along the way, we've received numerous honors. Some recent achievements include:
* Ranked in the top 20 U.S. journalism programs
* Most architecture awards among Northeast schools
* Winner of BigTech Corporation's industrial design contest in 1996
* Highest incoming SATs in tri-state region
* 23% minority enrollment among top on east coast

We welcome you to join North Atlantic in creating history!

5

7

Summary

In this lesson, you placed text from word processing files, and controlled the way it flowed from one page to the next. You threaded text manually and automatically, made multiple-column text frames, and broke and re-establish threads.

Lesson Review

4A How can you import text into an InDesign document?

Do you need to have a text frame on the page to import text into before using the Place command?

4B What key do you press as you place text to flow it semi-automatically?

What key do you press as you place text to flow it automatically?

4C   Name some advantages of placing text in a multiple-column frame.

Briefly describe how to break a thread to a frame.

When you delete one frame from a threaded series, does the text get deleted as well?

Colors, Swatches, and Gradients

Data Files
Recruitment Brochure. indd

Lesson Time
45 minutes

Overview

In this lesson, you will create colors, which you will use in the document for shading frames and coloring text. You will use different color models and save colors as swatches and tints, which you can easily apply to page elements. Additionally, you'll create gradients that blend between two or more colors.

Objectives

To effectively work with color models and apply colors within InDesign, you will:

5A **Define colors and swatches.**

You'll experiment with creating process colors using different color models, and will choose spot colors from a color library. You'll save colors as swatches, and will create a tint, or lighter variation, of a color.

5B **Define gradients.**

You'll define gradients that blend between two or more colors.

5C **Apply colors to fills and strokes of frames.**

You'll use the Toolbox and the Stroke palette along with the swatches you created to add fills and strokes to frames and type.

Topic 5A

Colors and Swatches

Process Colors

InDesign allows you to choose colors in a very straightforward and flexible manner. You will mix color components in one of several color models to form a color. Once the color is created, you can either apply it immediately to elements, or you can save the color with a name as a swatch for repeated use in the document. You will use the Color palette to define colors, and the Swatches palette to save and name them.

You can create colors with the Color palette using one of three models—RGB, CMYK, or LAB. A color model is a way of breaking a color into components, such as red, green, and blue.

The *RGB color* model combines red, green, and blue components to create colors, as shown in Figure 5-1. Your monitor uses red, green, and blue components to project the color to the screen. Red, green, and blue are called the primary additive colors, because when projected, as on your monitor, they combine to make white. You can choose red, green, and blue values from 0 to 255. You should typically use the RGB model for colors intended for display on screen or for output to a film recorder, since it's very easy to create vibrant RGB colors that aren't reproducible on a commercial printing press.

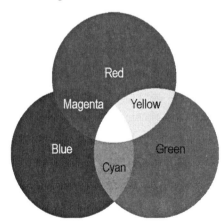

Figure 5-1: *Combining red, green, and blue.*

The CMYK (cyan, magenta, yellow, and black) color model uses four printing ink colors as components, as shown in Figure 5-2. Cyan, magenta, and yellow are referred to as the primary subtractive colors, since they combine together to form black (the absence of color), in theory. However, in reality, they combine to make a dark muddy purple, so black ink is added to solidify dark colors and to print pure black. *CMYK colors* can be specified using values from 0% to 100% of each ink color. You should typically use the CMYK model for colors in a publication that will be commercially printed, since the components match those used on a press.

You can open the Color Models.indd file in the Sample folder to view color versions of the following three color model and color wheel graphics.

RGB color:
A color model that defines colors by their red, green, and blue components. RGB is typically used for defining colors displayed on screen, since those are the phosphor colors used in monitors.

CMYK color:
A color model that defines colors by their cyan, magenta, yellow, and black components. CMYK is typically used to define colors for printing, since those are the ink colors used in most printers and presses.

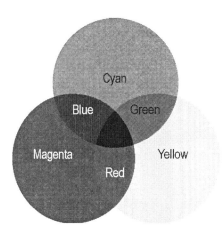

Figure 5-2: *Combining cyan, magenta, and yellow.*

The *LAB color* model defines colors mathematically, and is device independent, unlike RGB, which is used for monitors and scanners, and CMYK, which is used for printing.

LAB color, like RGB color, uses three components to represent color. L is the luminance component, ranging from black to white; A is a chromatic component ranging from green to red; B is a chromatic component ranging from blue to yellow.

The LAB color mode is used internally by InDesign when converting colors between image modes, such as from RGB to CMYK. It is also used by color management software that modifies images automatically to appear the same on different printers and monitors. Lastly, since it separates luminance from color, LAB color is also useful for changing a color's lightness without modifying the color.

You will experiment with different color models as you create colors. You may find Figure 5-3 helpful for visualizing how to mix colors using the RGB and CMYK models. Since the RGB and CMY components alternate around the wheel, you can mix the two nearest components from one model to get the color in the middle from another model. For example, in RGB, you can mix red and blue to get magenta.

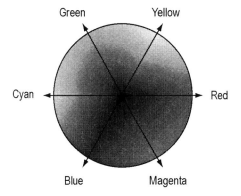

Figure 5-3: *Color wheel.*

LAB color:
A color model that defines colors by a luminance (brightness) component, as well as by two chromatic components (green to red balance, and blue to yellow balance). LAB color is typically used for displaying colors on a monitor and for color management software, since it has a wide gamut and is not defined based on any specific device.

You can also mix colors by thinking of one component to exclude. The colors red, green, and blue (R, G, and B) are the opposites of cyan, magenta, and yellow (C, M, and Y). So, for example, to mix a green color using the CMYK model, you would avoid using the opposite of green—magenta. A typical CMYK green color consists of cyan and yellow, but little or no magenta. Similarly, to mix a yellow color with the RGB mode, you would avoid using its opposite—blue. A typical RGB yellow consists of red and green, with little or no blue.

To mix colors, first display the Color palette. The Color palette lets you mix fill and stroke colors. The fill color is used for the interior of frames and for type; the stroke is used for borders around frames, outlined type, and lines. Specify a fill or stroke color by selecting the Fill or Stroke icon in the Color palette or Toolbox, so that the desired color icon appears in front. You can specify the color model (RGB, CMYK, or LAB) by choosing from the Color palette drop-down list. After specifying a color using any color model, you can view that color's closest approximation in the other color models by selecting a different color model from the Color palette drop-down list.

The RGB and LAB color models can create much brighter colors than can be printed with CMYK inks, since the CMYK color model has a narrower gamut, or range of reproducible colors. If you are choosing colors that will only be viewed on screen, such as for documents created for distribution on the World Wide Web, then you can safely use these models. However, for printing, you should generally use CMYK. If you select a LAB or RGB color that is not reproducible by the CMYK color model for printing, the Color palette displays an exclamation point, representing an out-of-gamut warning. You can click the exclamation point to revert the color to the closest CMYK approximation.

If you specify a fill or stroke color when no objects are selected, that color becomes the default fill or stroke color for any new objects you create. You can return to the original default colors (no fill, black stroke) by clicking the Default Fill And Stroke button in the Toolbox.

TASK 5A-1

Mixing CMYK Colors

Objective: To create colors for use in the document.

Setup: You will use the Recruitment Brochure.indd file.

1. You'll add colors to the North Atlantic University promotional brochure. **Open the Recruitment Brochure.indd file.**

2. You will first use the Color palette to mix colors. **Display the Color palette.**

3. You'll specify a fill color. **Click the Fill icon in the Color palette.** The fill color swatch is now in front of the stroke color.

4. Also, you should deselect all objects so the color you mix is not applied to anything on the page. **Choose Edit→Deselect All.**

5. You'll first experiment with mixing CMYK colors. From the Color palette drop-down list, **choose CMYK.** Four sliders appear; one each for the colors cyan (C), magenta (M), yellow (Y), and black (K).

6. **Experiment with dragging the three color sliders (C, M, and Y) to get different colors.**

7. You will now adjust the slider values to create a dark blue. **Drag the C slider all the way to the right so the value is 100%.**

8. You can also type values in the fields. In the M field, **type *60*.**

9. **Type *0* in the Y and K fields, then press Enter.** The color is now blue.

10. You'll now experiment with mixing RGB colors. From the Color palette drop-down list, **choose RGB.** You will create a bright vibrant green.

11. **Drag the G slider all the way to the right to a value of 255.**

12. **Drag the R and B sliders all the way to the left to values of 0.** A bright green is created. An exclamation point appears at the bottom left corner of the palette, indicating that this color is outside the gamut, or range of colors printable with CMYK inks.

13. You will convert this color to CMYK to see the nearest equivalent color, and what values would be used to create it. From the Color palette drop-down list, **choose CMYK.**

14. The color green is created in the CMYK color model by omitting the opposite color of green—magenta. The other ink colors are used, so green is created by combining cyan and yellow inks.

    You will also convert this color to LAB mode to see its component values. From the Color palette drop-down list, **choose LAB.**

15. **Drag the L slider all the way to the right to a value of 100.** The color becomes brighter, but remains green. This color is also outside the CMYK gamut, so the exclamation point appears at the bottom left corner of the palette. You will replace the color with the nearest printable one, shown in the small box to the right of the exclamation point.

16. **Click the exclamation point at the bottom left corner of the Color palette.** The color shifts to a darker, less vibrant green.

17. You intend to print this document, so you will work in CMYK from here forward. From the Color palette drop-down list, **choose CMYK.** The color is created almost entirely from cyan and yellow.

Swatches

When you have created a color you like, you can apply it directly to items such as frames or text. However, if you intend to use the color throughout the document, it is best to save it as a named swatch. Two advantages include consistency, because you know the color you are applying is defined the same way throughout the document, and flexibility—you can redefine a swatch color, and all of the elements you applied the color to change to match the new color. You will compile swatches in the Swatches palette.

InDesign CS's Swatches palette drop-down list offers commands to help manage swatches. You can use it to duplicate and delete swatches, as well as to add unnamed colors used in the document, select all unused swatches, and merge multiple swatches into one.

spot color:
A color that is printed using a single ink.

process color:
A color that is printed by combining cyan, magenta, yellow, and black inks, which are combined during the printing process.

To add the current color from the Color palette as a swatch, display the Swatches palette, then click its New Swatch button. A new swatch then appears in the Swatches palette, and is named with the ink percentages specified in the Color palette. You can edit a swatch by double-clicking it, then adjusting the color values in the Swatch Options dialog box. The swatch name will change dynamically with the color values you enter. In the Swatch Options dialog box, you can rename a swatch by unchecking the Name With Color Value check box, then entering a new name in the Swatch Name field. You can choose whether the color will print using the cyan, magenta, yellow, and black inks (referred to as *process color*), or by using one ink that has been pre-mixed to match the color you desire (*spot color*), by selecting from the Color Type drop-down list.

The icons to the right of each swatch in the Swatches palette indicate whether it is a process color, and which color model was used to create it, as shown in Figure 5-4.

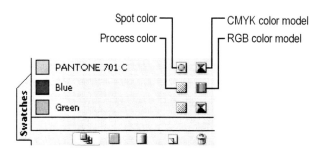

Figure 5-4: *The icons to the right of each swatch in the Swatches palette indicate its color model, and whether it is a process or spot color.*

TASK 5A-2

Creating Swatches

Objective: To create swatches for frequently used colors.

Setup: The Recruitment Brochure.indd file is open.

1. If necessary, **display the Swatches palette.**

2. The swatches palette already contains a few colors. You will add the current color, which you just created. In the Swatches palette, **click the New Swatch icon.** A new swatch, named with the ink percentages you chose, and colored green, appears in the Swatches palette.

3. You will edit the swatch. **Double-click the new swatch in the Swatches palette.** The Swatch Options dialog box appears.

4. Although the color is usable with any CMYK percentages, you'll round the values off to avoid trace amounts of magenta and black. **Type *60, 0, 75, and 0* in the C, M, Y, and K fields, respectively, then press Tab.** The color is now defined with round ink percentages, and the Swatch Name changed to match.

5. You'll now name the color with a descriptive name instead of using the ink values. **Uncheck the Name With Color Value check box.**

6. In the Swatch Name field, **type *Green*.**

Since you intend for this color to print using the CMYK inks as you designated, you'll make sure it prints as a process, not spot color. If necessary, **choose Process from the Color Type drop-down list.** You mixed the color using CMYK percentages, so the Color Mode is already set to CMYK.

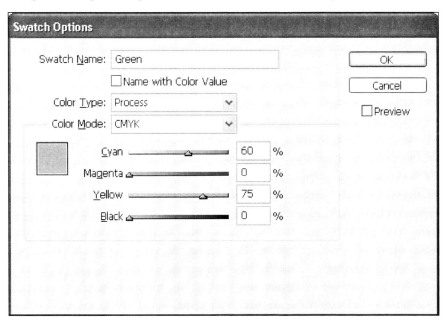

7. **Click OK.** The swatch is defined. The icons to the right of the color Green in the Swatches palette indicate that it is a process color, and that it was created with the CMYK color model.

Spot Colors

Unlike a process color, a spot color is printed from one pre-mixed ink. Ordinarily, you will select spot colors from a printed swatchbook, such as the PANTONE Formula Guide. This ensures that you know exactly how the color will print. However, since the printing inks are independent from the color model you use to choose a color, you can define a color using the CMYK or RGB color model, but specify that it print as a spot color. In general, it's not a good idea to define spot colors from those you've mixed using the screen as a reference, because the monitor, even if calibrated, will often not accurately represent the true ink color.

To make choosing a spot color simple, InDesign comes with several swatch libraries, allowing you to select colors from swatchbooks such as the PANTONE Color Formula Guide, the Trumatch Color Finder, and the TOYO Color Finder. When you create a swatch, you can easily choose one of those libraries from the Color Mode drop-down list, then type the color value corresponding to the printed swatch.

You can use the Color palette to define a color, but you specify whether the color should print as process or spot color via the Swatches palette. It's important that you understand the distinction between color models and printing inks when you create swatches, because for commercial printing in particular you should always know the total number of inks required for the print job. Many presses can only accommodate five or six inks at a time, so using seven or more inks in a publication would require two passes through the press, adding to the time and cost.

Also, composite printers can't accept spot color inks, so any colors you define as spot colors in InDesign will be simulated with the process colors on a desktop printer. This can result in significant color shifts from the color you intended, since some spot colors may be outside the printer's gamut. For example, the color PANTONE 300, a rich, saturated blue, can't be adequately printed on many desktop printers.

InDesign has three libraries for standard PANTONE colors; one is for use with coated paper, one for uncoated paper, and one for a matte finish. To use a color from a library, you first create a new swatch. If you choose New Color Swatch from the Swatch palette drop-down list, or hold down Alt as you click the New Swatch icon, the New Color Swatch dialog box immediately appears. You can choose the appropriate swatchbook from the Color Mode drop-down list. The Opening Swatch Libraries dialog box may appear for a moment, with a progress bar showing how much remains to be loaded. When it is complete, a list of swatchbook colors appears in the dialog box. When you select a PANTONE library, the colors are listed as a name or number followed by C if you're using the Coated library, U if using the Uncoated library, or M if using the Matte library.

Although you can't make a swatchbook color a process color while the swatchbook library is selected, you could choose CMYK or another mode from the Color Mode drop-down list to convert it, although the color itself may shift. For example, the nearest CMYK equivalent to PANTONE 647 C is 100C 56M 0Y 23K, but that may not appear the same when printed as it would using the pre-mixed PANTONE ink.

TASK 5A-3

Selecting PANTONE Colors

Objective: To create spot color swatches from libraries.

Setup: The Recruitment Brochure.indd file is open.

1. North Atlantic University has specified a blue color, PANTONE 647 as one of their logo colors; you'll now add this color to the document for use throughout. **Hold down Alt and click the New Swatch icon in the Swatches palette.** The New Color Swatch dialog box appears.

2. You can choose the appropriate swatchbook from the Color Mode drop-down list. From the Color Mode drop-down list, **choose PANTONE Solid Coated.**

3. **Scroll down the list to view some of the colors.**

4. When you know the swatch number, it is easiest to select it by typing it. In the PANTONE field, **type *647.*** The color, a medium blue, appears. Since this color library contains only colors that are intended for use as spot colors, Spot appears in the Color Type drop-down list and is grayed out so you can't change it to a process color while the library is still selected in the Color Mode drop-down list.

5. **Click OK.** A PANTONE 647 C swatch appears in the Swatches palette.

Tint Swatches

You may wish to use a lighter variation of colors you have defined as swatches. You can define these colors, known as tints, simply by dragging the Color palette's Tint slider to a lower percentage than 100. However, for consistency and flexibility, you can define specific tint percentages as swatches. For example, any item or swatch based on a swatch will change if you change the swatch definition, so you can easily modify either the original color swatch on which the tint is based, or a tint itself, and all of the items in the document that use the tint will reflect that change.

To create a tint of a swatch color, you first select the swatch in the Swatches palette, then from the Swatches palette drop-down list, select New Tint Swatch. In the New Tint Swatch dialog box, drag the Tint slider to specify the tint.

You can view the process color components of any color in the Swatches palette by positioning the mouse pointer on it and waiting a moment. Although spot colors won't use these ink components, you can see the nearest CMYK equivalent color. Since this works with tints as well, you can see the resulting CMYK values of a tint percentage applied to a process color.

TASK 5A-4

Creating Tint Swatches

Objective: To create colors that are lighter versions of existing swatches.

Setup: The Recruitment Brochure.indd file is open.

1. You will create two swatches of the blue PANTONE color you defined. **Click PANTONE 647 C in the Swatches palette.**

2. From the Swatches palette drop-down list, **choose New Tint Swatch.** The New Tint Swatch dialog box appears. The color PANTONE 647 C is selected at the top, and is grayed out, indicating that the tint you are creating must be a shade of that color.

3. **Drag the Tint slider to a value of 30%.**

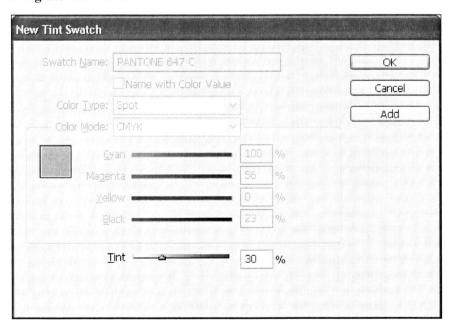

4. **Click OK.** A new swatch, titled PANTONE 647 C but with 30% to the right, appears in the Swatches palette. It is a lighter shade of blue than the original.

5. You will create another swatch. **Click the original color PANTONE 647 C in the Swatches palette. Be sure not to click the 30% tint you just created.**

6. From the Swatches palette drop-down list, **choose New Tint Swatch.** The New Tint Swatch dialog box appears.

7. In the Tint field, **type *15*.**

8. **Click OK.** A 15% tint of PANTONE 647 C appears in the Swatches palette.

9. **Choose File→Save.**

Topic 5B

Gradients

gradient:
A blend between two or more colors.

Gradients

InDesign allows you to create and apply *gradients* to items. You can create gradients using either the Swatches palette or the Gradient palette. As with creating tints, it's usually preferable to use the Swatches palette to create a gradient, because editing the swatch later will modify all of the gradients in the document to which it is applied.

To create a new gradient swatch, choose New Gradient Swatch from the Swatches palette drop-down list. The New Gradient Swatch dialog box appears, as shown in Figure 5-5. Type a name for the gradient, and choose a type. The two gradient types are linear and radial. A linear gradient progresses along a line, and a radial gradient progresses outward in a circle. You can then choose color by clicking on a color stop (a pointer beneath the gradient bar) and selecting either a named color or mixing a color by choosing a color mode and choosing color values. Each color stop represents one of the colors in the gradient. You can drag color stops to position the colors, and can control how quickly the color blends between color stops by dragging the diamond icon that is between them above the gradient bar. The diamond icon represents the midpoint between the two gradient colors, where the colors blend at 50%.

A gradient can have more than two colors; you can add a stop by clicking below the gradient bar. InDesign will create a stop color that doesn't change the appearance of the existing gradient. You can then modify the color of the new gradient stop. You can delete a gradient stop by simply dragging it away from the gradient bar.

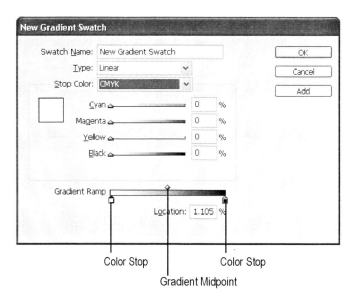

Color Stop   Color Stop

Gradient Midpoint

Figure 5-5: *You can create a gradient swatch using the New Gradient Swatch dialog box.*

Using the Gradient palette to create a gradient is similar, but you use the Color or Swatches palette to alter the stop colors. You can edit a stop color by clicking on it and changing the Color palette values to mix a color, or by holding down Alt and clicking on a color in the Swatches palette.

TASK 5B-1

Creating Gradient Swatches

    Objective: To create gradient swatches.

      Setup: The Recruitment Brochure.indd file is open.

1.   You'll now define a gradient swatch that you'll apply to a text frame on the cover of the brochure. You'll use the Swatches palette to define the gradient. From the Swatches palette drop-down list, **choose New Gradient Swatch.** The New Gradient Swatch dialog box appears.

You can click the Reverse button in the Gradient palette to switch the direction of a gradient.

If you want to blend between a process and a spot color, you can create a gradient from the process color to the Paper color, another between Paper and the spot color (running the opposite direction), overlay frames that have the two applied, and check the Overprint Fill check box in the Attributes palette with the topmost one selected. You can preview the effect of overprinting the gradients by choosing View→Overprint Preview.

2. You'll begin by experimenting with choosing colors. **Click the white color stop beneath the left side of the gradient bar in the New Gradient Swatch dialog box.**

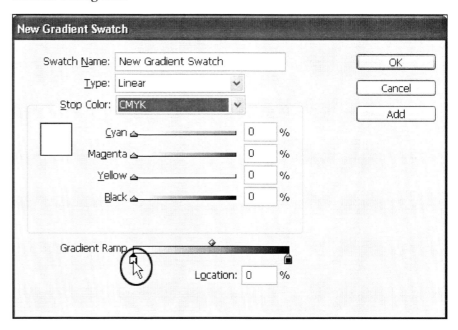

Since this stop was defined as a CMYK color, the Cyan, Magenta, Yellow, and Black sliders appear.

3. You will experiment with changing the colors of the gradient. **Drag the Yellow slider all the way to the right to a value of 100.** The left gradient color stop turns yellow, and the gradient blends from yellow to black.

4. **Click the color stop beneath the right side of the gradient bar.** Since the black color stop was defined as a named color, the existing swatch colors appear.

5. You can mix a color for this stop as well by choosing CMYK from the Stop Color drop-down list. From the Stop Color drop-down list, **choose CMYK.** The process color sliders appear.

6. **Drag the Black slider all the way to the left to a value of 0, and the Cyan slider all the way to the right to a value of 100.** The gradient now fades from yellow to cyan.

7. You'll add a third color stop. **Click below the gradient bar approximately ⅓ of the way across from the left.**

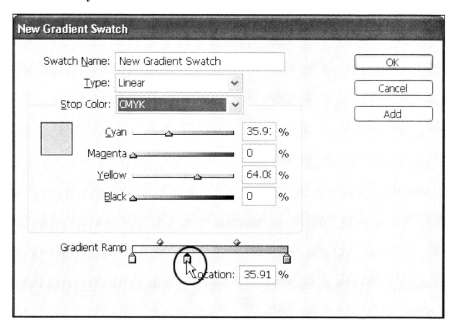

A third stop appears, with a Yellow value a bit higher than the Cyan value, representing the pre-existing gradient color where you clicked.

8. You will lengthen the fade from yellow to green at the left side of the gradient by moving the stop you just added. **Drag the middle color stop to the right so the Location value is approximately 60%.** More of the gradient is between yellow and green than between green and cyan.

9. **Drag the diamond that is above the gradient bar between the green and cyan stops to the left until the Location field reads approximately 20%.**

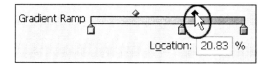

The gradient fades more rapidly from green to cyan.

10. You will remove the stop you added. **Drag the middle gradient stop down to remove it.** The gradient returns to blend only between the yellow and cyan stops.

11. Now that you've experimented with creating gradients, you'll define this one to blend from the green color you added to white. **Click the left gradient stop.**

12. From the Stop Color drop-down list, **choose Swatches.**

13. **Click Green.** The left stop color is green.

14. **Click the right gradient stop.**

15. You'll make the right stop a process color with 0% in all inks, so it acts as the paper color, which will be white in this case. **Drag the Cyan slider all the way to the left to a value of 0%.**

16. Lastly, you'll make the gradient transition more quickly to white. **Drag the diamond above the gradient bar to the left to a Location value of approximately 40%.** The center of the gradient is now lighter, since the transition from the solid color to the 50% tint is a shorter distance.

17. The gradient is now complete; you'll complete it by naming it. In the Swatch Name field, **type *Green to White.***

18. Click OK. The gradient swatch appears in the Swatches palette.

Topic 5C

Applying Fills and Strokes to Frames and Type

Once you have created a color by mixing one in the Color palette or by creating a swatch, you can apply it to the fill or stroke of a frame or type. To apply a color:

1. Select the object to which you want to apply color using the Selection tool, Direct Selection tool, or Type tool.

2. Click the Fill icon or Stroke icon in the Toolbox, Color palette, or Swatches palette.

3. If you selected a text frame with the Selection or Direct Selection tool, click the Formatting Affects Container or Formatting Affects Text icon in the Toolbox, Color palette, or Swatches palette to designate which one should receive the color.

4. Select a color, tint, or gradient using the Swatches, Color, or Gradient palettes.

5. Alternately, you can click the Apply Color, Apply Gradient, or Apply None buttons in the Toolbox to apply the most recently used color or gradient, or to remove the color or gradient.

You can also drag and drop color from the Swatches, Color, or Gradient palette to a frame's fill or stroke to apply it without having to select the object on the page first. Once a gradient is applied to an object, you can also drag across it with the Gradient tool to specify the direction and endpoints of a gradient, and can use the Gradient palette to specify its angle precisely or reverse its direction.

You can use the Formatting Affects Text button to apply color to text in a frame without selecting it with the Type tool, but only in a non-threaded frame.

If you wanted to apply a stroke to type, click the Stroke icon and select a color while the Formatting Affects Text icon is still selected.

TASK 5C-1

Applying Colors and Gradients

Objective: To apply color to fill and stroke frames.

Setup: The Recruitment Brochure.indd file is open.

1. You will now apply the blue PANTONE spot color to the sidebar frames. **Navigate to page 3.**

2. Since the right column of page three is a separate story from the one started on page two, you will color the frame blue to make the distinction clear to the reader. **Click the frame in the right column of page three.** Both the fill and stroke colors appear as slashes in the Toolbox, indicating that the frame is not filled or stroked with a color, but is transparent.

3. **Click the Fill icon in the Toolbox** to place it in front of the Stroke icon.

   Since this text frame is threaded to another one, you can't apply color to the text within using the Formatting Affects Text button; it will automatically apply to the frame.

4. **Click in the row containing PANTONE 647 C in the Swatches palette.** The frame fills with PANTONE 647 C.

5. This color is too dark, so you will use a tint instead. **Click in the row containing PANTONE 647 C 15% in the Swatches palette.**

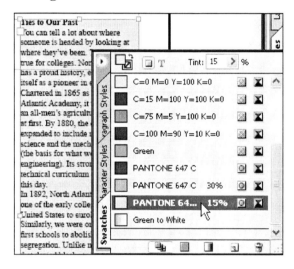

   The fill color is light enough to keep the text in the frame readable.

6. You will apply the same fill to the story's next frame on page seven. You will use a shortcut to move to the next frame in the thread. **Press Ctrl+Alt+Page Down.** Page seven, the page with the next threaded text frame appears, and the sidebar frame in the right column is selected.

7. **Click in the row containing PANTONE 647 C 15% in the Swatches palette.** The fill color is applied.

8. You will also apply color to text on the cover. **Navigate to page 1.**

9. You'll color the word "you" green. Using the Type tool, **select the word "you."** The Formatting Affects Text button is automatically selected, and the Fill box is still selected because you used it when filling the frames with color.

10. **Click Green in the Swatches palette, then click the pasteboard** to deselect the text. The word "you" is colored green.

11. You will put a thin stroke around the picture on the cover. This time, rather than using the Fill or Stroke icon in the Toolbox, you'll drag the color directly to the frame. You will apply a black stroke to the frame. Using the Selection tool, **drag the word Black in the Swatches palette to the top edge of the photograph containing the students, releasing it when the mouse pointer appears as a hand with a +.**

A black stroke is applied.

12. You will adjust the stroke weight. **Click the Stroke palette tab,** which is located in the group with the Color palette. The Stroke palette appears.

13. You will reduce the stroke from 1 point to ½ point. **Click the image on the page, then choose 0.5 pt from the Weight drop-down list.**

The stroke is now very thin. This keyline defines the edges of the picture clearly.

14. You'll apply a gradient to a frame with the words North Atlantic University and a fill and stroke to the text within without having to select the text with the type tool. **Click the words "North Atlantic University."** The frame is selected.

15. You'll first apply the gradient to the frame. If necessary, **click the Fill box and the Formatting Affects Container icon in the Toolbox.**

16. In the Swatches palette, **click Green To White.** The gradient applies to the frame's fill. Since the frame was rotated 90° counterclockwise, the gradient runs from bottom to top instead of left to right as it would ordinarily.

17. You'll now apply color to the type. In the Toolbox, **click the Formatting Affects Text icon.**

18. In the Swatches palette, **click PANTONE 647 C.**

19. You'll now change the direction of the gradient you applied to the frame. The Swatches palette also contains the Formatting Affects icons. In the Swatches palette, **click the Formatting Affects Container icon.**

20. While you specified the gradient's colors in the Swatches palette, you must use the Gradient palette to set the direction it flows in any frame in the document. **Click the Gradient palette tab,** which is in the group with the Stroke palette.

21. Since the frame itself is rotated 90°, the gradient is also rotated. You'll return the angle to 0° to make the gradient flow horizontally. **Type 0 in the Angle field and press Enter.**

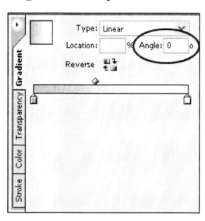

The gradient blends horizontally, with green on the left and white on the right.

Bleeds

bleed:
When an item extends beyond the page edge, so that when the page is printed on oversized paper and trimmed to size, the item's color will extend to the very edge. InDesign CS allows for separate bleeds on each side of the page of up to 6 inches.

When commercially printed, color pages are printed on paper stock that is larger than the page size, then the paper is trimmed to form the final pages. Since this process is somewhat imprecise, you should extend the colored areas a bit past the page edges, so a bit of color is cut off in the process. If you don't do this, the paper could be cut a bit oversize, and white gaps could appear at the edges. This process of extending the color past the page edges is called bleeding the color. Although you should ask your printer how much *bleed*, or extension past the page edges, is necessary, 1 pica (about .167 inches) should usually be sufficient.

TASK 5C-2

Specifying a Bleed

Objective: To specify a bleed.

Setup: The Recruitment Brochure.indd file is open.

1. You'll complete this frame by ensuring that the color will print all the way to the page edges.

   You will apply a 1 pica bleed to the text frame. As necessary, **zoom out so you can see a bit of the pasteboard above and below the page.**

2. **Drag the top middle frame handle up approximately 1 pica so the color bleeds past the page edge.**

3. **Drag the bottom middle frame handle down approximately 1 pica so the color bleeds past the page edge.**

You do not need to bleed the left page edge, because the brochure will be formed by folding sheets of paper that are twice the width of the page size. So, in this case, the last page (page eight) will be on the same side of one piece of paper as the cover (page one). If you chose to bleed color past the left edge, it would extend onto page eight when the document is printed.

4. **Click the pasteboard to deselect the frame, then click the Preview Mode icon in the Toolbox.** The bleeds and guides disappear, showing the page as it would look when printed and trimmed to size.

5. Lastly, you will reset the default fill and stroke colors to none. In the Toolbox, **click the Default Fill And Stroke icon.** The fill is set to none and stroke is set to black. However, you wish for frames you create in the future to have no stroke as well, so you will set it to none manually.

6. **Click the Stroke icon in the Toolbox, then click the Apply None icon.**

7. You will return to the fill icon so it is active for the next application of color. In the Toolbox, **click the Fill icon.**

8. You should return to the normal view to make editing easier. In the Toolbox, **click the Normal View Mode icon.** The bleeds and guides appear again.

9. **Save and close the file.**

Summary

In this lesson you created both process and spot colors as well as tints and gradients. You also saved each of these as swatches so they can be easily applied or edited later. You then used the swatches you saved to fill and stroke frames and type.

Lesson Review

5A What color model should you use to create colors if you are planning on getting a document commercially printed?

When is it best to use the RGB color model?

5B With which palettes can you create a gradient?

How can you add a new color stop to a gradient?

5C　How do you apply a color to the stroke of a frame?

How do you ensure that a filled frame bleeds to the edge of a printed page?

Formatting Type

Overview

In this lesson you will apply formatting to change the appearance of text. You'll identify the differences between character and paragraph formats, and will apply both. Lastly, you'll automate formatting by creating styles that hold paragraph or character formatting, then applying those styles quickly to bodies of text.

Data Files
Recruitment Brochure. indd

Lesson Time
45 minutes

Objectives

To format text, you will:

6A   Apply character formatting.

You'll format type with fonts, boldface and italics. You'll also add special characters and apply color to type.

6B   Apply paragraph formatting.

You'll distinguish paragraph formats from character formats, and will apply several paragraph formatting options. You'll adjust spacing between paragraphs, ensure that certain paragraphs stay together on a page, create tab settings to align text in tables, indent paragraphs, and create lines above or below paragraphs.

6C   Create styles to streamline formatting.

You'll define several formats at once as a style, then apply styles to paragraphs and characters in your document.

6D   Set text inset spacing.

You'll use text inset spacing to move text precisely within frames.

 # Topic 6A

Character Formatting

You can use character formatting to change fonts, sizes, and type styles. Character formatting can be applied to one character at a time, or to large bodies of text.

Font Types

You've probably used TrueType and Postscript fonts before. TrueType fonts are quite common. They have just one file, and can display and size without appearing jagged. However, most commercial printing providers prefer Postscript fonts because they are based on the same Adobe PostScript language as most high-resolution printing devices.

OpenType fonts contain many characters not available in other font types, including fractions, small caps, superscript and subscript characters, swashes, and more. Each OpenType font has just one file, which can be used for both Windows and Macintosh. When you apply an OpenType font to text, you can select from the following OpenType attributes:

* Ligatures, which are typographic characters used in place of specific letter pairs, such as "fi" and "fl."

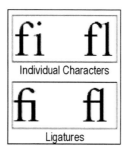

Individual Characters

Ligatures

* Fractions, which are typographic characters used in place of fractions typed as multiple characters.

* Ordinals, which are numbers such as 1st and 2nd, in which the letters are formatted as superscript.

* Swashes, which are alternate characters for capital letters, typically with ornamental, curving serifs.

* And more

Different options are available for different fonts. Options which are not available for the font you have selected are enclosed in brackets.

Basic Character Formatting

You already know how to apply basic character formatting using the Type menu, the Character palette, and the character formatting controls in the Control palette. The Character palette's options are shown in Figure 6-1. The character formatting controls in the Control palette include the same character formatting options.

When a font that is not installed in your system is applied to text, it appears with a pink highlight. This may happen when you open a document created by someone else using fonts you don't have, or when you apply a different font to text that doesn't have the same type styles as the font that was previously applied.

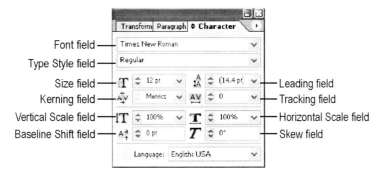

Figure 6-1: *You can apply character formatting using the Character palette.*

Character Formats	Description
Leading	Controls spacing between lines within a paragraph.
Kerning	Controls spacing between specific letter pairs.
Tracking	Controls spacing between all characters within a selection.
Vertical Scale	Controls the vertical size of characters independently from the horizontal size.
Horizontal Scale	Controls the horizontal size of characters independently from the vertical size.
Baseline Shift	Controls the vertical position of type relative to its default baseline.
Skew	Controls text skew amount, adding a "false italic" format to text.

You can also type a font name directly into the Font field in either the Character palette or the Control palette. If you type over the beginning of a font name, InDesign fills in the rest of the font name after you type the first few characters. This is often faster than choosing fonts from a long font drop-down list containing many fonts. If your computer has more than one font beginning with the letters you typed, InDesign inserts the first one alphabetically. After typing a font name, you can press Tab to move to the Type Style field, then type the first letters of the type style you want. For example, type I for italic.

You can type a font size into the Size field in increments of 0.001 points, from .1 to 1296.

TASK 6A-1

Changing Font and Size

Objective: To apply font and size changes to characters of text.

Setup: The Recruitment Brochure.indd file is open.

1. You will now perform additional character formatting for the recruitment brochure. You will begin by changing the typeface of one of the text stories. If necessary, **open the Recruitment Brochure.indd file.**

2. **Double-click the page numbers 2-3 in the Pages palette.**

3. Using the Type tool, **click in either column on page two.** An insertion point appears in the text.

4. The text, which retained formatting from the imported word processing documents, is set in several typefaces and sizes. You will change the entire story to one typeface and size. **Choose Edit→Select All.** InDesign selects all of the text in the story. All of the text in the entire document except for the history sidebar, the headlines, and the page numbers, is selected.

The Adobe Garamond Pro font is located alphabetically in the Font menu by Garamond, not by Adobe.

5. Using the Character palette, **specify Adobe Garamond Pro, Regular.** All of the type changes to the same font.

6. You will set all of the type to the same size as well. From the Size drop-down list, **choose 10.**

7. You decide to make the font a little larger. **Type *10.25* in the Size field in the Character palette, then press Enter.** All of the text in the story is now formatted as Adobe Garamond Pro, 10.25 point.

8. **Select the text Join Our Quest in the left column on page two.**

9. **Double-click the word Adobe in the Font field of the Character palette to select the word.**

10. **Begin to type Arial into the Font field in the Character palette, and continue to type the word Arial until that font appears in the Font field.**

11. **Press Tab to move to the Type Style field, then type *B*.** The Bold type style is selected.

12. Since the typeface Arial appears larger than Adobe Garamond Pro, you will make the heading type size smaller to compensate. **Type *9* in the Size field, then press Enter.** The heading changes typeface and size. Later, after all of the character and paragraph formatting is complete, you will format each of the other headings the same way.

Leading

Leading is the measurement of space between the baseline of one line and the baseline of the next line, as shown in Figure 6-2. By default, the text in a document uses *auto leading*. Auto leading creates a leading value of 20% larger than the largest type size on a line. Therefore, if the largest type size on a line is 10 points, the leading would be 12 points (20% larger than 10 points). If the largest type size in a line is 50 points, auto leading would produce a leading value of 60 points (20% larger than 50 points). When auto leading is in use, the leading value appears in the Leading field within parenthesis. This lets you know that the leading value will adjust automatically if the type size changes.

leading:
The vertical distance between the baselines of two lines of type.

auto leading:
Leading set automatically by InDesign; by default auto leading is set to 120% of the type size.

When you decide on a college, you're making one of the biggest decisions of your lifetime. Where you choose to attend school will greatly influence your career, your social life, your world view, your location, your earning potential, and your outlook on life.	When you decide on a college, you're making one of the biggest decisions of your lifetime. Where you choose to attend school will greatly influence your career, your social life, your world view, your location, your earning potential, and your outlook on life.
Auto leading for 10 pt type (Leading value of 12 pt)	Increased leading for 10 pt type (Leading value of 15 pt)

Figure 6-2: *Leading is the measurement of space between baselines of text within a paragraph.*

If you are using large initial caps or other text formatting that changes the size of the text, auto leading may produce unintended results. If you had more than one font size in a block of text, each line would not use the same amount of space. To avoid this problem, you can set a fixed leading amount.

To adjust the leading, select the paragraphs whose leading you want to change, then enter a value in the Leading field in the Character palette or Control palette. The Control palette displays type formatting settings when the Type tool is selected.

TASK 6A-2

Adjusting Leading

Objective: To adjust type leading.

Setup: The Recruitment Brochure.indd file is open.

1. In this story, most of the text uses auto leading, but the opening text has custom line spacing that was applied in the word processing document you imported. You would like each line in the main story to have a leading value of 12 points. **Choose Edit→Select All.** The entire story is selected.

2. In the Control palette, **select 12 pt** from the Leading drop-down list.

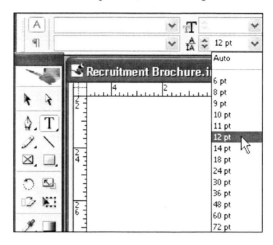

The story reflows to adjust to the new leading.

3. **Click within the selected text to deselect it.**

4. **Save the file.**

Special Characters & Glyphs

InDesign and other programs allow you to type characters that aren't visible on the keyboard. To produce these special characters, you can hold down Alt as you type a four-digit number on the numeric keypad. You can also see how to produce these characters using the Character Map accessory.

If you begin dragging to select text from outside the frame, you may accidentally create a new frame. Therefore, you may find it easiest to select text at the left edge of a column by dragging across it from right to left, rather than left to right.

However, it is often inconvenient to look up the keystrokes for typing characters. InDesign has two ways for you to access special characters. First, you can use the Type→Insert Special Character command. The submenu allows you to insert symbols such as bullets, copyright symbols, special spaces and hyphens, and page numbering codes.

Second, you can use Type→Glyphs to open the Glyphs palette for inserting special characters. Glyphs are alternate forms of a specific character. For example, in a given font, each uppercase letter may be available in varying forms, such as a swash version or a small cap version. You can use the Glyphs palette to insert characters from any of the fonts you have installed on the computer. In the Glyphs palette, the characters with a small triangle in the lower right corner have available alternatives.

TASK 6A-3

Inserting Special Characters and Glyphs

Objective: To create special characters quickly.

Setup: The Recruitment Brochure.indd file is open.

1. In this document you would like to have a bullet (•) appear for the paragraphs in the Career Choices section on page five. In the Pages palette, **couble-click the Page 5 icon.**

2. You will zoom in to get a closer look at the characters. **Hold down Ctrl and the Spacebar.**

3. **Click in the middle of the right column on page five as many times as necessary to view the document at 200% magnification.** The page zooms in so you can see the character in more detail.

4. **Select the first asterisk character, located to the left of Agriculture and Natural Resources.**

5. You will now replace it with a bullet. **Choose Type→Insert Special Character→Bullet Character.**

6. You will look for an interesting alternative to a round bullet character. **Select the bullet character you just created.**

7. **Choose Type→Glyphs.** The Glyphs palette appears.

8. **Scroll through the palette to see the available characters.** As you can see, the Adobe Garamond Pro font, since it is an OpenType font, contains many characters you usually don't see in other fonts.

9. You can insert a character from any of the fonts on your computer. You will insert a character from a picture font. From the Font drop-down list at the bottom of the palette, **select Webdings.** Each of the characters in the font appears. It is very convenient to select a character using this dialog box, since you do not have to know what character to type to get the symbol.

The Glyphs palette is an installed plug-in. Plug-in modules add features to InDesign. Many plug-ins, including this one, come with InDesign, and are automatically installed in the Plug-Ins folder. Many InDesign features are provided by plug-ins. This makes it easy to upgrade or remove specific parts of the program just by replacing or removing a plug-in, or to add new plug-ins, created by Adobe or other software developers.

If you type words in a foreign language, you can select them, then choose that language from the Language drop-down list in the Character palette, so InDesign properly hyphenates and spell checks them.

10. You can enlarge the display of the symbols to make it easier to select one. **Click the Enlarge button to enlarge the display of the characters, if necessary.**

11. You will find a right-pointing triangle to replace the round bullet. **Scroll to view the triangle shapes.**

12. Double-click the right-pointing triangle.

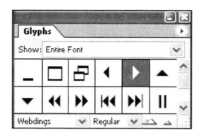

13. You will copy and paste this triangle to replace the other asterisks. **Select the right-pointing triangle you just created.**

14. Choose Edit→Copy.

15. Select the asterisk in the following line of text.

16. Choose Edit→Paste.

17. You can replace the remaining asterisks by pasting; you do not need to copy the triangle again because it remains on the clipboard until you copy or cut something else. **Select each asterisk in this column, and paste the triangle to replace them.**

Formatting with OpenType Fonts

You can choose to view instances where InDesign automatically substituted glyphs in your type by checking the Substituted Glyphs check box in the Composition panel of the Preferences dialog box.

As you have seen, Open Type fonts contain many characters that aren't available in other fonts. In this document, you would like to use some fractions. You will take advantage of OpenType's ability to create true fractions and change some of the text to fractions. You can locate typographic alternatives for characters using the Glyphs palette by choosing Alternatives For Selection from the Show drop-down list.

TASK 6A-4

Creating True Fractions with OpenType Fonts

Objective: To format text as a fraction.

Setup: The Recruitment Brochure.indd file is open.

1. You will change the text 3/4 to a fraction. **Select the text 3/4 above the bulleted list.**

2. Scroll in the Glyphs palette to locate the fraction 3/4.

3. **Double-click the ¾ fraction in the Glyphs palette.** InDesign replaces the text with a true fraction.

4. **Close the Glyphs palette.**

Topic 6B

Paragraph Formatting

Unlike character formatting, paragraph formatting must be applied to entire paragraphs of text at a time. For example, since choosing to boldface text is a character format, you can make one character in a word boldface. However, when you indent text, a form of paragraph formatting, you are affecting an entire paragraph. You cannot indent one character of text without affecting the rest of the paragraph. When using paragraph formatting, it is not necessary to select every character in the paragraph. You can click anywhere in the paragraph, and the formatting will affect the entire paragraph. If you are formatting multiple paragraphs simultaneously, you only need to select a portion of the paragraphs you are formatting.

You will use paragraph formatting to set the space between paragraphs, breaks before paragraphs, indents, rules, and tabs. You can apply paragraph formatting using the Paragraph palette, or the Control palette, when it displays the paragraph formatting controls. To access the paragraph formatting controls in the Control palette, you must first select the Type tool, then click the Paragraph Formatting Controls button at the far left of the Control palette.

The Paragraph palette contains the options shown in Figure 6-3. The paragraph formatting controls in the Control palette includes the same Paragraph formatting options.

If a fraction you need isn't available, you can create your own by choosing the numbers in the Glyphs palette.

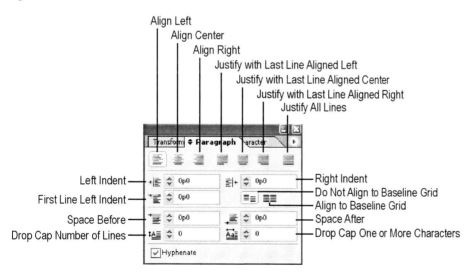

Figure 6-3: *You can apply paragraph formatting using the Paragraph palette.*

Paragraph Spacing

Instead of typing an extra paragraph break between paragraphs, you should add space before or after paragraphs using paragraph formatting. This approach is more flexible and makes it easier to control the paragraph spacing. It also eliminates the possibility of leaving blank lines at the tops or bottoms of columns, which could happen if you simply typed extra paragraph break characters.

TASK 6B-1

Setting Paragraph Spacing

Objective: To add space between paragraphs.

Setup: The Recruitment Brochure.indd file is open.

1. You will add 1 pica (12 points) of space after all paragraphs in the body text story. **Click in the left column of the body text.**

2. **Choose Edit→Select All.** The entire story is selected.

3. You will format it with the Paragraph palette. **Click the Paragraph palette tab in the group with the Character palette.**

4. **Type *1* in the Space After field, then press Enter.** Since picas are the default units, you do not need to type 1p. Each paragraph now has one pica of space following it. However, any paragraphs that fall at the bottom of a text frame will not have space applied after them; they are allowed to extend to the bottom of the frame.

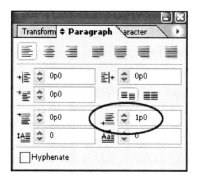

5. You will change the paragraph spacing before and after headings as well. **Click to place the insertion point in the heading Join Our Quest on page two.**

6. In the Space Before field, **type *1*.**

7. In the Space After field, **type _0_.**

8. Press Enter.

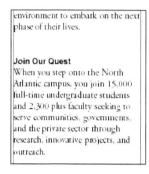

There is a two-pica gap above the paragraph, which is generated (one from the paragraph above, one from its own formatting), but no gap below it. Therefore, the heading stands out, but is clearly associated with the following text.

Keep Options

Widows and _orphans_ are unattractive, and make the document harder to read (particularly when the following text is on the next page). You can also use paragraph formatting to specify that a certain number of lines in a paragraph will be kept together; this will prevent widows and orphans.

To specify keep options, choose Keep Options from the Paragraph palette drop-down list, or from the Control palette drop-down list, when it displays the paragraph formatting controls. You can either keep all of the lines in a paragraph together, or specify the number of lines that must be in the same column. In most cases, it is not necessary to keep the entire paragraph together; you just wish to avoid widows and orphans. You can also specify that a particular paragraph automatically keep with the next paragraph. This is often applied to headings to prevent a heading from appearing at the bottom of a column with the next paragraph in another column or page. Lastly, you can use keep options to force paragraphs to begin a new column or new page.

widow:
A single line at the top of a column.

orphan:
A single line at the bottom of a column.

TASK 6B-2

Setting Keep Options

Objective: To control how paragraphs are kept together on a page.

Setup: The Recruitment Brochure.indd file is open.

1. You would like to prevent widows and orphans in all of the body text paragraphs. **Choose Edit→Select All.**

2. From the Paragraph palette drop-down list, **select Keep Options.** The Keep Options dialog box appears.

3. **Check the Keep Lines Together check box.**

4. If necessary, **select the At Start/End of Paragraph option.**

5. In the Start and End fields, **type 2.** As necessary, InDesign will move a paragraph that is split between columns to fit entirely in the second column to ensure that a minimum of two lines of the paragraph appear in any column.

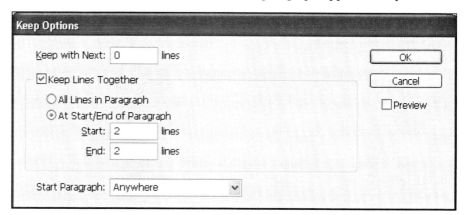

6. **Click OK.** Although none of the paragraphs in the current spread are affected now, you will see this formatting take effect as you continue to format text, because no widows or orphans will appear.

7. You will ensure that headings keep with the next paragraph. **Click to place the insertion point in the heading Join Our Quest on page two.**

8. From the Paragraph palette drop-down list, **select Keep Options.** The Keep Options dialog box appears.

9. In the Keep With Next field, **type 1.** The heading must appear in the same column as the next line. Since each body text paragraph contains 2 in the Start field under Keep Lines Together, the heading and the following paragraph would be moved to the next column if two lines in the paragraph do not fit at the bottom.

10. **Click OK.** Again, you cannot see the effect of the Keep with Next attribute, but it acts as a safeguard to prevent problems if text is reflowed later. You will apply this same formatting to all of the headings in a later section.

11. You will move text that belongs under Head to Head Action on page four into place. You will begin by removing the small Head to Head Action heading from the body text, since it appears as a headline on the next spread. **Triple-click in the text Head to Head Action on page three, then press Delete.**

12. The following paragraph belongs on page four. You could move it there by pressing Enter several times. However, if you did that, there would be either too many or too few paragraph break characters if the text were reformatted. **Click in the paragraph that begins with "We know that going to college isn't all about academics...," following the paragraph you just deleted.**

13. From the Paragraph palette drop-down list, **select Keep Options.** The Keep Options dialog box appears.

14. In addition to the settings you already specified, you will make the paragraph begin at the top of a page. From the Start Paragraph drop-down list, **choose In Next Column.** You could also have chosen On Next Page; either will move the text to the next column in the story's thread of frames, which happens to be on the next page. Choosing In Next Column will not move the text to the right column on page three, because the sidebar frame that exists there is not threaded to the current story.

15. **Click OK.** The text moves to the following pair of pages.

16. You will move another paragraph to the next page to put it under Heading for Success... In the right column of page five, just before the Research Opportunities heading, **click in the paragraph that begins with We take great measures to ensure that each North Atlantic student's experience is a success story.**

17. From the Paragraph palette drop-down list, **select Keep Options.**

18. In addition to the settings you already specified, you will make the paragraph begin at the top of a page. **Select On Next Page from the Start Paragraph drop-down list, then click OK.** The text moves to the following spread. The text in each spread now reflects the headline accurately.

19. **Save the file.**

Tabs

Unlike typewriters, computers use proportionally spaced fonts. For example, on a computer, the uppercase letter W takes up much more space than the lowercase letter i. Therefore, you cannot use spaces to line up text. Even if text looks approximately lined up on the screen, the spacing may look uneven when printed or if you zoom in to a fairly high magnification. Instead, you should use tabs to line up text.

InDesign has four types of tab stops: Left-justified, Center-justified, Right-justified, and Decimal tabs. Setting a left-justified tab stop causes any text you type after the tab to line up flush left with the left tab stop. Setting a center-justified tab stop causes any text you type after the tab to center on the tab stop. Setting a right-justified tab stop causes any text you type after the tab to line up flush right with the tab stop. Setting a Decimal tab stop causes the decimal point of numbers (or another character you specify in the Align On field) to line up with the tab stop.

If you create an extra tab stop, you can remove it by dragging it away from the Tabs palette.

To set tab stop positions, choose Type→Tabs. The Tabs palette appears, displaying a ruler and tab type icons, shown in Figure 6-4. You can align the Tabs palette with the column of text so that the tab ruler aligns to the text, as long as you can see the top of the frame. To align the Tabs palette with the text, click the Position Palette Above Text Frame button. Select the type of tab you want to use, then click the ruler to set the tab position. You can then drag the tab stop to adjust its position along the ruler. You can also type in a position for the tab in the X field. You can change the tab type of a selected tab stop by selecting a different tab icon.

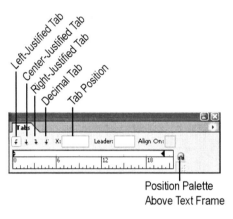

Position Palette
Above Text Frame

Figure 6-4: *The Tabs palette displays a ruler and icons for setting tab stops.*

TASK 6B-3

Creating Tab Settings

Objective: To line up text neatly in tabular form.

Setup: The Recruitment Brochure.indd file is open.

1. You will use tab stops to align the text in the High Standards section on page six. **Double-click the page numbers 6-7 in the Pages palette to view the spread of pages six and seven in the window.**

2. You should zoom in on the text you wish to format to get a clearer view. **Hold down Ctrl+Spacebar, and click the word Enrolled in the left column of page seven until the magnification is 200%.**

3. First you will change the font and reduce the size of the text in the table so it will stand out from the surrounding text and fit between the margins without being crowded. **Select the text from SAT through 25%. Be certain to select all of the characters, not just some of them.**

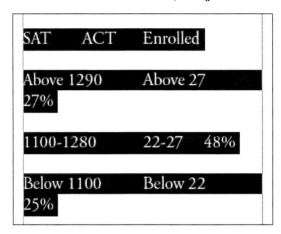

Since you will first perform character formatting, you must select all of the characters.

4. In the Control palette, from the Font drop-down list, **select Arial.**

5. From the Size drop-down list, **select 8 pt.**

6. You can now set tab stops to control the spacing within the paragraphs. **Choose Type→Tabs.** The Tabs palette appears, with a ruler and tab type icons.

7. **Scroll up so the top of the column frame is visible, at the top margin guide, not the guide at 9p6.**

8. **Click the Position Palette Above Text Frame button** 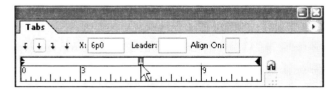**.** The palette's ruler aligns with the text frame.

9. First you will set a center tab stop at 6p. If necessary, **scroll down so you can see all of the selected text.**

10. **Click the Center Justified Tab button** in the **Tabs palette.** The zero point on the ruler is at the left edge of the text frame the table is contained in, not the left edge of the page.

11. **Click just above the ruler at 6p to set a center tab stop.**

12. The text after the first tab character lines up with this new tab stop. However, it is a bit too close to the SAT text to its left. **Drag the Center tab stop you just created to the right until the X field reads 6p9.** The ACT text is moved further to the right.

13. You will create a second tab stop for the right column of text. **Click the ruler at approximately 10p.** A new center tab stop is positioned at 10p.

14. You will right align the text in the last column. In the Tabs palette, **click the Right Justified Tab button** . The text in the right column of the table is right justified.

15. You will move the text near to the right margin. **Drag the Right tab stop you just created to the right until the X field reads 11p7.** The Enrolled text lines up with this new tab setting. You have finished setting tabs for the table.

SAT	ACT	Enrolled
Above 1290	Above 27	27%
1100-1280	22-27	48%
Below 1100	Below 22	25%

16. Save the file.

Indents

It is often necessary to change the position of text from the left and right margins. Although you can sometimes achieve the desired appearance by adding spaces, tab characters, and extra paragraph breaks, it is most convenient to move text from the margins with indent formatting. By applying formatting instead of typing extra spaces, you gain much finer control of the indenting, and it is easier to remove later if so desired. In addition, applying indent formatting allows you to apply indents to multiple paragraphs at once.

If the top of the column is visible when you open the Tabs palette, it will automatically align with the top of the text frame.

Block and First-Line Indenting

You can specify indent settings using the indenting fields in the Paragraph palette, or the in the Control palette when it displays the paragraph formatting controls. In addition, you can specify indents using the indent controls in the Tabs palette, shown in Figure 6-5. Drag the indent controls to specify first line, left, and right indent settings.

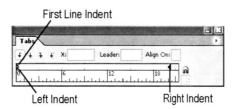

Figure 6-5: *You can specify indents using the indent controls in the Tabs palette.*

TASK 6B-4

Setting Indents

Objective: To apply block and first-line indenting.

Setup: The Recruitment Brochure.indd file is open.

1. You will experiment with block and first-line indents to learn how to create them. **Double-click the page 2 icon in the Pages palette.**

2. You should zoom back out to see the effect of the indents on the whole page. **Choose View→Fit Spread In Window.**

3. **Position the mouse pointer in the first body text paragraph in the left column.**

4. **Drag down to select part of the first and second paragraphs.** As with any paragraph formatting, you do not need to select the entire paragraph to perform indenting.

5. **Click the Position Palette Above Text Frame button.** The Tabs palette is positioned at the top of the frame.

6. You will change the left and right indents to create a block indent. **Drag the bottom triangle at the left side of the Tabs palette ruler to the right until the X field value is 2p8.**

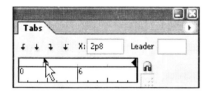

The text is indented on the left. You'll now view the indent settings in the Control palette.

7. At the left edge of the Control palette, **click the Paragraph Formatting Controls button.**

The paragraph formatting controls appear. The Left Indent field is set to 2p8.

8. You will now add a right indent. **Drag the triangle at the right side of the Tabs palette ruler to the left until the X field value is approximately 2p8.** If it does not allow you to drag to 2p8, drag to approximately 2p8.5.

The paragraphs are indented from both the right and left sides, giving the appearance of being placed in a narrower column.

9. You will remove the block indent formatting and apply first-line indenting to try another option. **Drag the bottom left triangle all the way to the 0 mark in the Tabs palette ruler.**

10. **Drag the right triangle all the way to the right in the Tabs palette ruler.**

11. **Drag the top left triangle to the right until the X field value is 1p0.**

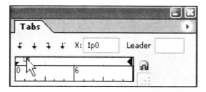

The First Line Left Indent field in the Control palette, which specifies the distance the first line is indented relative to the rest of the paragraph, is set to 1p0. The first line of each paragraph is indented by 1 pica.

12. You will remove the indents from these paragraphs. **Drag the top left triangle all the way to the 0 mark in the Tabs palette ruler.** You have removed the indenting from the opening paragraphs.

Hanging Indents

You will typically format bulleted and numbered paragraphs to line up as hanging indents. In a hanging indent, the first line of a paragraph is to the left of the other lines in the paragraph. A hanging indent is used to line up bulleted or numbered paragraphs so that the main text lines up to the right of the bullet or number. To create hanging indents, specify a first line indent that is to the left of the left indent, as shown in Figure 6-6. In addition, you must add a tab character following the hanging character to ensure that the text following the hanging text in the first line aligns with the following lines of text.

As an alternate approach, you can specify a hanging indent by entering the indent values in the Left Indent and First Line Indent fields in the Paragraph palette or Control palette.

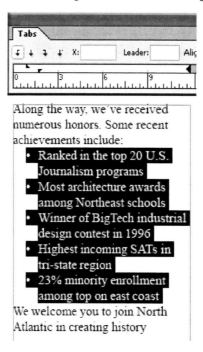

Figure 6-6: *In a hanging indent, the first line of a paragraph is to the left of the other lines in the paragraph.*

As you adjust tabs and indent settings, you may benefit from viewing the document's hidden characters. For example, you can view hidden characters to verify that a tab character follows text you will format as a hanging indent. To view hidden characters, choose Type→Show Hidden Characters. Light blue characters will then appear throughout the text. Paragraph breaks are represented by ¶s; spaces are indicated by small dots, and each tab character is represented by →.

TASK 6B-5

Setting Hanging Indents

Objective: To apply hanging indents.

Setup: The Recruitment Brochure.indd file is open.

1.   You will format the bulleted paragraphs in the Career Choices section to line up as hanging indents. **Double-click the page 6 icon in the Pages palette.**

The bulleted paragraphs in the right column of page six are too spread out. You will first remove the extra space between paragraphs. You can select several paragraphs by Shift clicking, much as you selected multiple frames by Shift clicking earlier.

2.   **Click in the Agriculture and Natural Resources paragraph, hold down Shift, then click in the Journalism paragraph.** All of the text between the two places you clicked is selected. Since you will apply a paragraph format, it is not important to select each word in the paragraphs.

3.   In the Control palette, **type _0_ in the Space After field, then press Enter.**

The extra space is removed from between the paragraphs. You will now create the hanging indents. As the text is formatted now, several paragraphs wrap beneath the bullet on the first line. The hanging indent formatting will remedy this problem.

4.   **Choose Type→Show Hidden Characters.** Each of the paragraphs you wish to apply the hanging indent to have a tab (→) character between the triangle and the following text, so the hanging indents will work correctly.

5.   **Select the bulleted paragraphs in the Career Choices section on page six, including Life Sciences.**

6.   To set a hanging indent, you will apply a left indent with the bottom triangle in the Tabs palette ruler, then drag the top triangle back to the left. **Click the Position Palette Above Text Frame button.** The palette's ruler aligns with the text frame.

7.   **Drag the bottom triangle in the Tabs palette to the right until the X value is 1p6.** The text is left indented.

8. **Drag the top triangle in the Tabs palette to the left until the X value is -1p0.** By dragging the top triangle, you adjusted the first line indent. This moved the triangular bullets to the left in the selected paragraphs.

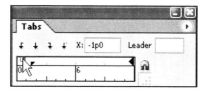

The text in the first line of each paragraph that follows the triangular bullet is indented to 1p6, as is the text in all of the remaining lines of the paragraph. The text aligns, so the hanging indent is complete.

9. You no longer need to use the Tabs palette. **Close the Tabs palette.**

10. **Save the file.**

Rules

Rules are lines that appear either above or below paragraphs. A typical use for rules is above or below headings to make them stand out from the surrounding body text. The advantage of using a paragraph rule instead of drawing a line with a line tool is that a rule will move with a paragraph as the text flows within a document.

To add rule formatting, select Paragraph Rules from either the Paragraph palette drop-down list, or the Control palette drop-down list when the paragraph formatting controls are displayed. Specify the rule settings in the Paragraph Rules dialog box, shown in Figure 6-7. You can move a rule above or below its default baseline by setting an offset value. You can enter an offset either as an absolute value or as a percentage of the distance to the next line of text.

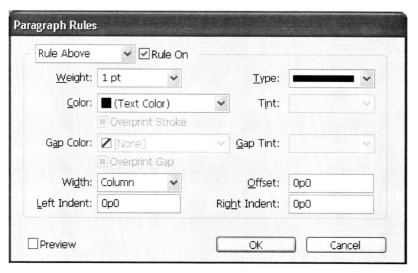

Figure 6-7: *Specify paragraph rule settings in the Paragraph Rules dialog box.*

TASK 6B-6

Creating Rules

Objective: To create horizontal lines that appear above or below paragraphs.

Setup: The Recruitment Brochure.indd file is open.

1. You will add a rule beneath the top line of the table you formatted using tabs. You will use a shortcut to scroll while an insertion point appears as you use the Type tool. **Hold down Alt.**

2. **Drag to view the text you added tabs to earlier (SAT, ACT, Enrolled).**

3. **Hold down Ctrl+Spacebar, then click the text SAT ACT Enrolled as many times as necessary to view the document at 200% magnification.** Before adding a rule, you will remove the extra space between the paragraphs as you did for the bulleted text on page six.

4. **Select the text from SAT to the paragraph beginning 1100-1280.**

5. In the Control palette, **type *0* in the Space After field, then press Enter.** The space is removed from after each paragraph except for the last one in the table.

6. You will now add a paragraph rule beneath the top line. **Click in the line beginning SAT.**

7. With the paragraph formatting controls displayed in the Control palette, from the palette's drop-down list, **choose Paragraph Rules.** The Paragraph Rules dialog box appears.

8. You will add a rule below the paragraph. From the Rule Type drop-down list, **select Rule Below.**

9. **Check the Rule On check box.**

10. **Check the Preview check box.** The rule appears directly beneath the baseline of the text.

11. You will move the rule 2 points below the baseline. **Type *0p2* in the Offset field, then press Tab.** The rule is moved down from the baseline.

12. Currently, the rule extends all the way to the margin. Since the text stopped at the right tab stop you set, you will change the length of the rule to match. From the Width drop-down list, **choose Text** to make the rule the width of the text. The text stops at the right edge of the text.

13. Lastly, you will change the width of the rule. **Type *1.5* in the Weight field, then press Tab.** The rule is thicker, and you have finished formatting it.

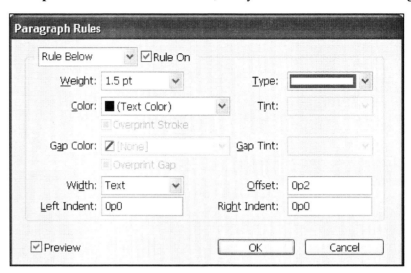

14. Click OK.

15. Save the file.

Topic 6C

Styles

You will often apply certain types of formatting repeatedly in a document. Although you can manually format each instance, doing so is tedious, and you are likely to format them inconsistently.

Instead, you can use styles to format text more quickly and consistently. When you create a style, you define a combination of formatting choices. You can then apply this formatting to selected text in one step instead of several.

InDesign allows you to create both character and paragraph styles. Character styles include only character attributes, such as font, size, and type style. Paragraph styles include both the character and paragraph formatting in a paragraph. So, for example, when you apply a paragraph format, the font, size, type style, leading, indenting, and space between paragraphs could all be changed at once. This greatly speeds up repetitive formatting.

If your document contains text formatted with the attributes you want to use in a paragraph style, you can select some of the text, open the Paragraph Styles palette, then click the palette's Create New Style button. A new style is created based on the formatting of the selected text. You can then apply that style to any paragraph by selecting one or more paragraphs and selecting the new style from the Paragraph Style palette. After applying a style to a paragraph, if you then modify the formatting of the text in the paragraph, then a + appears after the style name in the Paragraph Styles palette. This indicates that the paragraph uses the style, along with additional formatting.

Rather than basing a style on existing text, you can create a style and specify its settings using only the Paragraph Styles palette. To create a new style, from the Paragraph Styles palette drop-down list, select New Paragraph Style, or hold down Alt and click the Create New Style button. The New Paragraph Style dialog box then appears. Select formatting categories on the left side of the dialog box to access formatting options for the new style, and specify a name for the style. You can also use the Shortcut field to define a keyboard shortcut for applying the style quickly. You can use any of the numeric keypad number keys (with NumLock on) plus any combination of the Ctrl , Alt, and Shift keys. After creating a style, you can modify it at any time by double-clicking the style's name in the Paragraph Styles palette to access the Paragraph Style Options dialog box.

TASK 6C-1

Defining Paragraph Styles

Objective: To define paragraph styles, which can later be applied to format entire paragraphs at once.

Setup: The Recruitment Brochure.indd file is open.

1. Since paragraph styles are more inclusive, you will usually need more of them than character styles. You will begin by creating a paragraph style for the headings. **Navigate to page 2, and display it at fit page magnification.**

2. You have formatted the heading Join Our Quest in the left column with both character formatting (font, type style, size, leading) and paragraph formatting (space before and after, keep lines together, keep with next line). You will save this formatting as a style to apply to the other headings in the story. **Double-click the word Quest in the heading in the left column.**

3. **Click the Paragraph Styles palette tab.** The Paragraph Styles palette appears. The palette indicates that the selected paragraph is formatted with the Normal style.

You can copy formatting from one paragraph to another using the Eyedropper tool. To copy formatting, click the Eyedropper tool, then click the text that has the formatting you would like to copy. To apply the formatting to other text, select the text using the Eyedropper tool. You may apply the formatting as many times as you want after copying it once. However, unlike styles, when you change the formatting for the original paragraph, the formatting will not automatically change for all paragraphs whose formatting you copied from the original paragraph.

You can also create a new paragraph style by selecting New Paragraph Style from the Control palette drop-down list, when the paragraph formatting controls are displayed. You can modify the current paragraph style by selecting Style Options from the Control palette drop-down list.

4. You will create a new style based on the selected text. **Click the Create New Style button at the bottom of the Paragraph Styles palette.** A new Paragraph Style 1 appears in the palette. The Normal+ style is still selected, however, because although you used the selected text to define a new style, it is not automatically applied.

5. **Click Paragraph Style 1 in the Paragraph Styles palette.** The formatting does not change, because the style was defined based on the selected text.

6. You will change the style name to make it more descriptive. **Double-click Paragraph Style 1 in the Paragraph Styles palette.** The Paragraph Style Options dialog box appears.

7. In the Style Name field, **type *Heading.***

8. You will use the shortcut Shift keypad 1 for applying this style. **Click in the Shortcut field.**

9. **Press Shift and type 1 on the numeric keypad.** The shortcut appears as Shift + Num 1.

10. The character and paragraph formats you applied are all listed. You will slightly increase the type size. **Click Basic Character Formats.**

11. In the Size field, **type *9.25.*** You are finished setting the formatting for the Heading style.

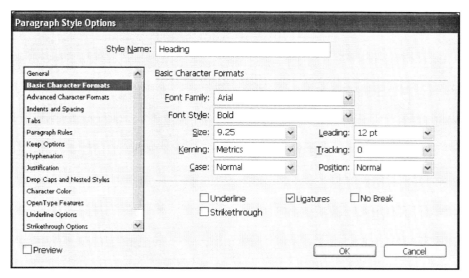

12. **Click OK.** The style name changes to Heading in the Paragraph Styles palette, and the words Join Our Quest are enlarged very slightly.

Paragraph Style Application

When applying paragraph styles, you do not need to select the entire paragraph; it will apply to the entire paragraph containing the blinking insertion point. You can apply styles by selecting them in the Paragraph Styles palette or the Control palette (when it displays the paragraph formatting controls) or by pressing the style's shortcut, if you specified one.

TASK 6C-2

Applying Paragraph Styles

Objective: To apply paragraph styles you have created to text in the document.

Setup: The Recruitment Brochure.indd file is open.

1. You can now apply the style to the other heading paragraphs to perform all of the formatting at once. **Click in the paragraph with the words Our Credentials.**

2. **Click Heading in the Paragraph Styles palette.** All of the character and paragraph formatting for the heading changes at once.

3. You will apply the Heading style to the next heading by using the shortcut. **Click in the paragraph with the words Our Facilities.**

4. **Press Shift+1, using the 1 key on the numeric keypad.** The Heading style is applied to the paragraph.

5. You can use either approach to format the remaining headings. **Apply the Heading style to the remaining headings in the body text story, except for the SAT ACT Enrolled heading to the tabular information you formatted earlier and the heading for the GPA Enrolled tabular information.**

   You were able to format the headings much faster using paragraph styles than you would have been otherwise.

The heading titles are: Our Incoming Freshmen, Sporting Events, Fraternities & Sororities, Culture, North Atlantic Student Center, Action Off Campus, The Surrounding Region, Research Opportunities, Be a Big Fish, Career Choices, and High Standards.

Character Styles

Paragraph styles apply both paragraph and character formatting to entire paragraphs. You may wish to apply only character formats to a body of text, and you may wish to have that formatting applied only to selected text, rather than to entire paragraphs at a time. For example, you might want a way to quickly emphasize certain words in a paragraph by changing the font, type style, and size. You can use character styles to perform this kind of formatting.

You can create character styles using the same techniques you used to create paragraph styles, except that you will use the Character Styles palette rather than the Paragraph Styles palette. You can also create, modify, and apply character styles using the Control palette, when it displays the character formatting controls.

 TASK 6C-3

Creating Character Styles

Objective: To create styles that can be applied to specific characters within a paragraph instead of to the entire paragraph.

Setup: The Recruitment Brochure.indd file is open.

1. The table you formatted earlier contains character formatting that you would like to apply to other tables, but you do not wish to apply the tab settings to other paragraphs with a different number of tabs. You will create a character style to quickly duplicate the font and size elsewhere in the document. If necessary, **double-click the page 7 icon in the Pages palette.**

2. **Select the word "above" in the second line of the table you created with tab settings.**

3. You will create the style based on the selected text much as you did with the paragraph style you defined. **Click the Character Styles palette tab in the group with the Paragraph Styles palette.**

4. You can use a shortcut to allow you to name the style as you create it. **Hold down Alt, and click the Create New Style button in the Character Styles palette.** The New Character Style dialog box appears.

5. In the Style Name field, **type *Table Text.***

6. You used Shift plus a number for the paragraph style you created; you will use a different modifier key for character styles to distinguish them. In the Shortcut field, **hold down Ctrl, then type 1 on the numeric keypad.** The shortcut is listed as Ctrl + Num 1. The settings are complete.

7. **Click OK.**

8. You can now apply this formatting to other text in the document. **Navigate to page 3.**

9. There is a small table on page three that needs the Table Text character formatting. **Select the text from GPA Enrolled through 1%.** You must select each individual character to which you want to apply the character style.

10. **Click Table Text in the Character Styles palette.** All of the selected text is changed to Arial 8 point formatting. However, the paragraph formatting that was applied to the other table of information, including tab settings and space before and after, was not applied to this text, because you wish to create tab settings specific to these lines.

11. You have used paragraph and character styles to make repetitive formatting much easier. **Save the file.**

Topic 6D

Text Inset Spacing

By default, frames allow text to extend to the very edges. This is typically desirable, particularly in instances in which the text frame has a transparent or white background. However, when you have applied color to the frame, it is useful to move the text in from one or more of the sides, so it does not appear to crowd the frame edges. You can achieve this by applying text inset spacing. If you did not know how to use text inset spacing, the alternative would be to create a second, larger frame behind a text frame to add color. However, this is awkward and unnecessary.

Since text inset spacing is an attribute of the frame, and not of individual characters or paragraphs within the frame, you must use the Object→Text Frame Options command to set the inset value. You can then move the text in from each side (left, right, top, and bottom) of the frame separately using the fields in the Inset Spacing section.

TASK 6D-1

Setting Text Insets

Objective: To move text away from one or more edges in a colored frame.

Setup: The Recruitment Brochure.indd file is open.

1. The text in the History text story is too close to the edges of the text frame. You will specify a text inset to move the text in from the edges of the text frame. **Navigate to page 3.**

2. **Click the light blue text frame on the right side of the page.**

3. **Choose Object→Text Frame Options.** The Text Frame Options dialog box appears.

4. **Check the Preview check box.** You will now see the changes as you make them.

5. In the Inset Spacing section, **type *p10* in the Top field.** Be certain not to type 10p by accident.

6. **Press Tab.** The text moves away from the top of the frame. You will set the other three inset values to match.

7. **Type _p10_ in the Left, Bottom, and Right fields, pressing Tab after each.** The text is moved in from all edges of the frame.

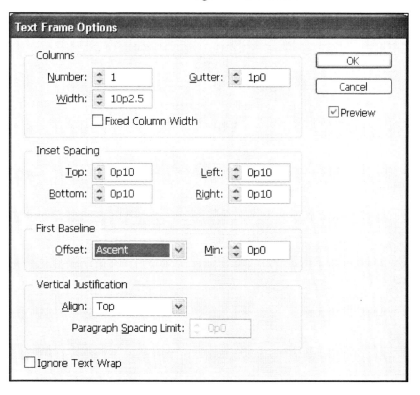

8. The text looks much better than when it extended to the edges of the frames. The inset spacing is complete. **Click OK.** You should apply the same inset value to the light blue frame on page seven.

9. **Navigate to page 7.**

10. **Click the light blue text frame on the right side of the page.**

11. **Choose Object→Text Frame Options.** The Text Frame Options dialog box appears.

12. **Type _p10_ in each of the fields in the Inset Spacing section, pressing Tab after each. Click OK.** The text is moved in from all edges of the frame.

13. **Save the file.**

Suggested Time:

10 minutes

Apply Your Knowledge 6-1

Character and Paragraph Formatting

You will practice character and paragraph formatting.

1. Go to page three.

2. Remove the space after the paragraphs from GPA Enrolled through 1%.

3. Create a right tab stop at 11p7 for these paragraphs.

4. Create a rule below the top line of the GPA Enrolled table with an offset of 2 points, the width of the text, and 1.5 point weight.

5. Select the entire Ties to Our Past sidebar story on pages three and seven.

6. Format the text as Arial, 9 point, 12 point leading, 1p space after.

7. Apply the Heading paragraph style to the title Ties to Our Past.

8. Remove the space after each of the bulleted paragraphs on page seven in the History story except for the last one.

9. Apply hanging indent formatting to all of the bulleted paragraphs, with a 1p left indent and -1p first-line indent.

10. Select the headline at the top of page two, apply a fill color of Green, and use it to define a paragraph style called Page Title, with a shortcut of Shift keypad 2.

11. Apply the Page Title style to the headlines on pages two, four, and six.

12. Edit the Heading style to change the character color to PANTONE 647 C. (Hint: select a heading paragraph before double-clicking the style name to avoid applying the style to another paragraph inadvertently).

13. No longer display the Hidden Characters.

14. Save the document.

15. Close the document.

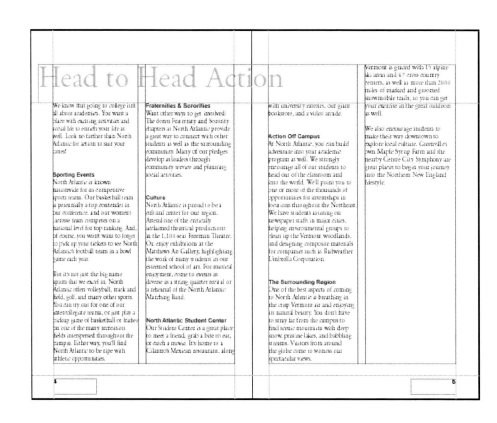

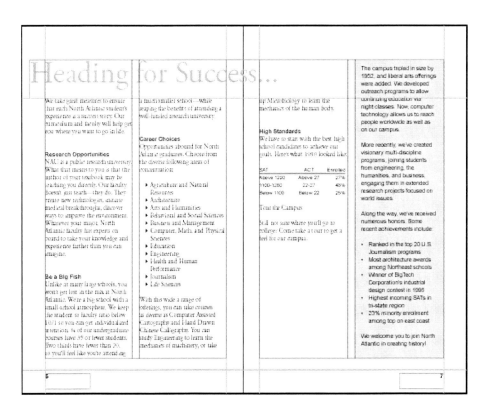

Heading for Success...

We take great measures to ensure that each North Atlantic student's experience is a success story. Our curriculum and faculty will help get you where you want to go in life.

Research Opportunities
NAU is a public research university. What that means to you is that the author of your textbook may be teaching you directly. Our faculty doesn't just teach—they do. They create new technologies, initiate medical breakthroughs, discover ways to improve the environment. Whatever your major, North Atlantic faculty list experts on board to take your knowledge and experience farther than you can imagine.

Be a Big Fish
Unlike at many large schools, you won't get lost in the mix at North Atlantic. We're a big school with a small-school atmosphere. We keep the student to faculty ratio below 18/1 so you can get individual attention. ¾ of our undergraduate courses have 35 or fewer students. Two thirds have fewer than 20, so you'll feel like you're attending

a much smaller school—while reaping the benefits of attending a well-funded research university.

Career Choices
Opportunities abound for North Atlantic graduates. Choose from the diverse following areas of concentration:

- Agriculture and Natural Resources
- Architecture
- Arts and Humanities
- Behavioral and Social Sciences
- Business and Management
- Computer, Math, and Physical Sciences
- Education
- Engineering
- Health and Human Performance
- Journalism
- Life Sciences

With this wide a range of offerings, you can take courses as diverse as Computer Assisted Cartography and Hand Drawn Chinese Calligraphy. You can study Engineering to learn the mechanics of machinery, or take

up Microbiology to learn the mechanics of the human body.

High Standards
We have to start with the best high school candidates to achieve our goals. Here's what 1998 looked like:

SAT	ACT	Enrolled
Above 1290	Above 27	27%
1100-1280	22-27	48%
Below 1100	Below 22	25%

Tour the Campus

Still not sure where you'll go to college? Come take a tour to get a feel for our campus.

The campus tripled in size by 1952, and liberal arts offerings were added. We developed outreach programs to allow continuing education via night classes. Now, computer technology allows us to reach people worldwide as well as on our campus.

More recently, we've created visionary multi-discipline programs, joining students from engineering, the humanities, and business, engaging them in extended research projects focused on world issues.

Along the way, we've received numerous honors. Some recent achievements include:

- Ranked in the top 20 U.S. Journalism programs
- Most architecture awards among Northeast schools
- Winner of BigTech Corporation's industrial design contest in 1996
- Highest incoming SATs in tri-state region
- 23% minority enrollment among top on east coast

We welcome you to join North Atlantic in creating history!

5   7

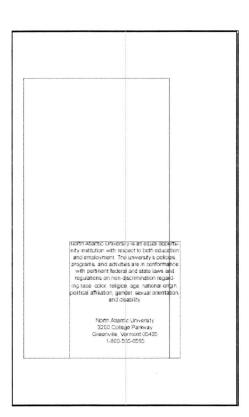

North Atlantic University is an equal opportunity institution with respect to both education and employment. The university's policies, programs, and activities are in conformance with pertinent federal and state laws and regulations on non-discrimination regarding race, color, religion, age, national origin, political affiliation, gender, sexual orientation, and disability.

North Atlantic University
3200 College Parkway
Greenville, Vermont 05405
1-800-555-6565

Summary

You have applied different types of formatting to text to change its appearance and how it flows from page to page. You saw how some paragraph formats, such as space between paragraphs and indenting, are better alternatives than typing extra characters into text. And you made formatting much faster by creating paragraph and character styles, which let you apply several formats with one click or keyboard shortcut.

Lesson Review

6A Name a fast way to change fonts without choosing one from a menu.

Why does using autoleading sometimes cause formatting problems?

6B What are widows and orphans?

How can you avoid widows and orphans

6C Why is using styles more efficient than manually formatting type?

Briefly describe the two techniques for creating styles.

6D When is it important to apply text inset spacing?

How do you specify text inset spacing?

Graphics and Layout

Data Files
Recruitment Brochure.
indd
Football.jpg
Slam Dunk.jpg
Classroom.eps
Study.tif
Lab.psd
Conversation.jpg
Catalog.indd
Magazine Ad.indd
French Ad Copy.indd

Lesson Time
45 minutes

Overview

You have placed graphics on a page, cropped them, and resized them. You will expand on that knowledge, getting more control over precise size, positioning, and appearance. You'll also control how text flows around graphics, adjusting the distance the text stays away from rectangular text frames as well as creating irregular text wraps around images. You'll use layers to make it easier to manipulate overlapping items.

Objectives

To control graphics, you will:

7A   **Place and manipulate graphics.**

You'll place graphics both into existing frames, and by creating a frame automatically as you import. You'll control the display resolution of imported images, resize graphics at the same time as the surrounding frame, and will fit graphics to match the size of the frame they're in. As you place the images, you'll learn a bit about some of the graphic file formats InDesign accepts.

7B   **Control text wrap around graphics.**

You'll adjust the text wrap distance around rectangular frames, and will create irregular wraps around graphics.

7C   **Create and manage layers.**

You'll add layers that you can show or hide to organize the page content and allow multiple versions of items for different purposes.

Topic 7A

Placing and Manipulating Graphics

InDesign offers a variety of techniques for placing graphics. You can place a graphic so that a frame is automatically created, or you can create a frame first, then place the graphic into that frame. You can also place a graphic so that it replaces an existing, selected graphic. Lastly, you can control the resolution of the on-screen display of images.

InDesign supports a variety of graphic file formats. Therefore, you can obtain images from a variety of sources, such as from a scanner, a paint application, an illustration application, or the Internet. Some of the common graphic file formats InDesign supports include:

- *EPS (Encapsulated PostScript)* and *TIFF (Tagged Image File Format)* files, which are typically used for print publications, and can hold high-resolution color images. Both can hold images in either the RGB or CMYK color

EPS graphic:
A graphic saved in the EPS (Encapsulated PostScript) format. EPS files can hold Bézier curve-based (vector) graphics as well as raster images (pixel-based images such as photographic images), and are typically created by applications such as Adobe Photoshop, Adobe Illustrator, Macromedia FreeHand, or CorelDraw.

TIFF graphic:
A graphic saved in the TIFF (Tagged Image File Format) format. TIFF files can hold only raster images (pixel-based images such as photographic images), and are typically created by applications such as Adobe Photoshop or scanner software.

model. Although either can be used for printing, the CMYK model is generally preferable for printing to a press because it uses the ink colors for color components.

- *GIF* and *JPEG* format images, which are frequently used for displaying images on the World Wide Web, because both can compress files to small sizes for fast downloading. GIF (Graphic Interchange Format) images must be 256 or fewer colors, so they are not usually suitable for print. JPEG (Joint Photographic Experts Group) images can be millions of colors, but are compressed significantly, sometimes resulting in a very visible loss in quality. When used for the Internet, images in either format are lower resolution than is preferable for printing. Internet images are typically 72 to 100 pixels per inch (ppi, sometimes also called dots per inch, or dpi), whereas printed images should usually be between 200 to 300 ppi. However, the JPEG format can be used for high resolution images intended for print, since JPEG supports CMYK as well. JPEG images prepared for print should be created with a small amount of compression applied, to avoid distorting the image.

- Photoshop and Illustrator graphics, which are often created for use in InDesign documents. You can import native Photoshop and Illustrator files into InDesign. This allows for great flexibility, because Photoshop and Illustrator files frequently contain editing information, such as layers and channels, that would be lost when saving to other formats. If you import a Photoshop or Illustrator file directly into InDesign, you can edit the graphic with the application you used to create it, save it, and return to InDesign, where the changes you made will be applied.

GIF graphic:
A graphic saved in the GIF (Graphic Interchange Format) format. GIF files can hold only raster images (pixel-based images such as photographic images) with up to 256 colors, and are typically created by applications such as Adobe Photoshop or web graphics applications.

JPEG graphic:
A graphic saved in the JPEG (Joint Photographic Experts Group) format. JPEG files can hold only raster images (pixel-based images such as photographic images), and are typically created by applications such as Adobe Photoshop, scanner software, or digital cameras.

Graphic Replacement

When placing an image, you may want it to replace an existing image in the document. To replace an existing image, select the existing image, then choose the Place command. In the Place dialog box, check the Replace Selected Item check box, then select the new image and click Open. Checking this check box will cause the placed graphic to replace the graphic in the selected frame. Unchecking this check box will cause a loaded graphic mouse pointer to appear when you place the graphic, whether or not a frame is selected when you place the graphic. After replacing a graphic, you can choose the Undo command to return the replaced graphic to the frame. The mouse pointer will then appear as a loaded graphic icon, so you can click elsewhere to place the new graphic.

TASK 7A-1

Placing Graphics

Objective: To place graphics into new and existing frames.

Setup: The Recruitment Brochure.indd file is open.

1. You will import photographs of people on campus to add interest to the recruitment brochure. You will begin by placing two pictures of athletes. If necessary, **open the Recruitment Brochure.indd file.**

2. **Navigate to page 4.**

You will place the pictures on the pasteboard, since you do not have a plan for where to put them on the pages yet. Since you do not have a pre-determined size for these pictures, you will let InDesign create the frames around them automatically. You should deselect all page elements first.

3. **Choose Edit→Deselect All.**

4. **Choose File→Place.** The Place dialog box appears.

5. You will place a picture of a football player first. **Click Football.jpg.** This is a JPEG file, which has been compressed to a very small file size. However, unlike most JPEG files saved for the Internet, it was saved with a relatively high resolution (225 ppi), which makes it suitable for printing.

6. **Click Open.** The loaded graphic mouse pointer appears.

7. You can now place the image wherever you want. You will place the image on the pasteboard. **Click to the left of the page title (Head to Head Action) on the left pasteboard.** The picture appears in a new frame that exactly fits the image size.

8. If necessary, **use the Selection tool to drag the picture to the left so it does not touch the page.**

9. You will now place another picture on the pasteboard, replacing the current picture. If necessary, **click the picture** to select the frame.

10. **Choose File→Place, then select the Slam Dunk.jpg image.** This is also a JPEG file, saved at a reasonable resolution for printing.

11. If necessary, **check the Replace Selected Item check box.**

12. **Click Open.** Instead of a loaded graphic mouse pointer appearing, the picture is imported into the frame that was selected when you chose the Place command. You decide to keep both graphics in the file.

13. **Choose Edit→Undo Replace.** The football player image returns to the frame. In addition, you now have the loaded graphic mouse pointer, so you can place the basketball player image on the pasteboard into a new frame.

14. **Click below the football player on the pasteboard.** The basketball player picture appears in its own frame, which is fit to the image.

15. If necessary, **use the Selection tool to drag the picture to the left so it does not touch the page.**

16. You will place one more picture on the pasteboard for future use. This time, you will avoid placing the image into an existing frame by deselecting all frames first. **Choose Edit→Deselect All.**

17. **Choose File→Place, then select Classroom.eps.** This is an EPS file; as mentioned earlier, EPS files are usually intended for printed output.

18. **Click Open.** The loaded graphic mouse pointer appears.

19. You will place the image on the pasteboard. **Click below the picture of the basketball player on the pasteboard.** The picture appears in a new frame that exactly fits the image size.

20. It would make more sense to put this picture on the next spread of pages, which mentions academics and personalized attention. You can move items from the pasteboard of one page to another simply by dragging them. Using the Selection tool, **drag the picture straight down until the mouse pointer is at the very bottom of the window; continue to hold down the mouse button.** The window begins to scroll down, and the next spread will move into the window.

21. **Release the mouse button once the picture is on the pasteboard of the next spread of pages (pages six and seven).** You will position the three pictures you have placed on their pages later.

Graphic Frames

If you know the size of the graphic frame you wish to place a picture in, you can create it before placing the picture. You can create the frame using one of the shape or frame tools in the Toolbox. To place a graphic within the existing shape, select the frame, select the Place command, check the Replace Selected Item check box, then place the graphic.

It's also useful to create frames ahead of time when making template documents, in which you want to designate the placement of text or graphics, but want to allow different content to be used each time a publication is created from the template. If you wish to clarify that a certain frame should contain a graphic, you can use the Rectangle Frame tool instead of the Rectangle tool, because the Rectangle Frame tool creates a frame with an X in it. This would cue the person creating the document that a graphic should be placed in that frame. You would use the Rectangle tool to create any frames you intended to hold text, since this tool does not create the X.

Picture Display Quality

When you place a graphic, the version you see on screen is only a placeholder, or proxy image that roughly represents the image you placed. This onscreen proxy version may appear at a much lower resolution than the actual print version. InDesign uses the original high resolution version of the image for printing. However, you can change the resolution of the onscreen version of an image.

For example, you may want to show images at a lower resolution to improve performance. On the other hand, you may want to display images at a higher resolution to get a better preview of how they'll appear when printed. Although specifying a higher display quality improves an image's appearance onscreen, it also makes the document much slower to work with. So, you should choose whether you would like to see the image better or have better performance.

To adjust an image's display quality, select the graphic, then choose from the Object→Display Performance submenu. This submenu is also available in a shortcut menu when you right-click a graphic.

TASK 7A-2

Placing Graphics within Frames

Objective: To specify graphic frame settings before placing pictures.

Setup: The Recruitment Brochure.indd file is open.

1. You will create graphic frames in the columns of pages two and three, in which you will then place pictures. **Double-click the page numbers 2-3 in the Pages palette.**

2. You wish to place a picture of a student studying at the bottom left corner of page two. Since you know ahead of time that the image should fit exactly to the left column width, you will create a frame ahead of time. **Select the Rectangle Tool.**

3. **Position the mouse pointer at the bottom left margin on page two.**

4. **Drag up and to the right to create a rectangular frame that is one column wide and approximately 8 picas tall. Use the Transform palette for reference as you drag.** The frame overlaps text in the column, but you will address this problem with a text wrap in a later section.

5. You will resize the frame to make it exactly 8 picas tall. You want the bottom edge to stay where it is, at the bottom margin. **Click the bottom-left proxy point in the Transform palette.**

6. **Type *8p* in the H field in the Transform palette, then press Enter.** The frame is exactly 8 picas tall, and the bottom edge stays at the bottom margin.

7. You will now place a graphic in the frame. **Choose File→Place, then select Study.tif, then click Open.** The picture appears in the frame. However, it appears very blocky, with very little detail.

8. You will now show the image at a higher resolution. **Zoom in on the image at 150%.**

9. **Choose Object→Display Performance→High Quality Display.** The image displays at a much higher resolution.

10. Using the Direct Selection tool, **hold down the mouse button on the picture for a few moments, then drag the picture up slightly within the frame.** InDesign's dynamic graphics preview allows you to see the entire image as you drag so you can position it precisely.

11. If you plan to place more graphics, you should deselect the frame before doing so. **Click the pasteboard to deselect all frames.**

12. Although this is not a template document, you will use the Rectangular Frame tool to practice with it. **Select the Rectangle Frame tool.**

13. You will now create the frame on page three. If necessary, **scroll to the right to view the bottom of the left column on page three.**

14. **Position the mouse pointer at the intersection of the bottom and left margins on page three.**

You may wonder why the pictures of the athletes or the picture of the classroom didn't look as blocky as the one of the student. The reason is that InDesign displays a proxy image for any image that is greater than 48k in file size. When smaller images are placed, InDesign displays the actual image. The athlete images were smaller than 48k because of the JPEG compression that was applied. Although the classroom image is larger than 48k, it is an EPS image. Unlike files in other formats, EPS images contain their own 72 ppi proxy image, which is automatically used when the image is placed in desktop publishing applications such as InDesign.

15. Drag up and to the right to create a rectangular frame that is one column wide and approximately 12 picas tall. This frame has an X in it because you created it with the Rectangle Frame tool.

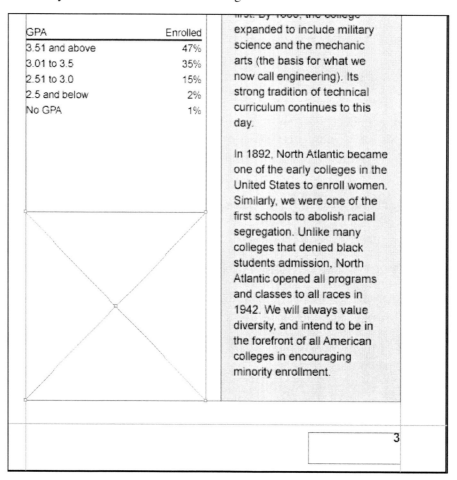

GPA	Enrolled
3.51 and above	47%
3.01 to 3.5	35%
2.51 to 3.0	15%
2.5 and below	2%
No GPA	1%

...first. By 1880, the college expanded to include military science and the mechanic arts (the basis for what we now call engineering). Its strong tradition of technical curriculum continues to this day.

In 1892, North Atlantic became one of the early colleges in the United States to enroll women. Similarly, we were one of the first schools to abolish racial segregation. Unlike many colleges that denied black students admission, North Atlantic opened all programs and classes to all races in 1942. We will always value diversity, and intend to be in the forefront of all American colleges in encouraging minority enrollment.

3

If the X does not appear in the frame you just created, choose Show Frame Edges from the View menu.

16. You will resize the frame to make it a specific height, using a bottom proxy point to keep the bottom of the frame in place. **Click the bottom-left proxy point in the Transform palette.**

17. Type *12p* in the H field in the Transform palette, then press Enter. The frame is exactly 12 picas tall, and the bottom edge stays at the bottom margin.

18. You will now place a graphic in the frame. **Choose File→Place, then select Lab.psd.** This is a Photoshop file. Unlike many other applications, InDesign lets you place native Photoshop files, without requiring you to save them in another format first.

19. Click Open. The picture appears in the frame at 72 ppi. You have finished placing graphics for now.

20. Save the file.

Graphic and Frame Manipulation

You can use several commands to change the way images fit within their frames. However, you cannot access these commands when the frame's contents are selected with the Direct Selection tool. You must select the frame itself with the Selection tool. You can fit a graphic in its frame with commands from the Object→Fitting submenu. These same commands are available in a shortcut menu when you right-click a graphic frame.

Earlier, you cropped a graphic by dragging the frame's corner handles to resize the frame. Rather than cropping a graphic using this technique, you can resize a frame and resize the graphic along with it by holding down Ctrl as you drag the frame's handles. To resize the picture without distorting its proportions, you can hold down Shift, along with Ctrl, as you drag a frame handle.

TASK 7A-3

Manipulating Graphics and Frames

Objective: To control the placement and size of graphics within their frames.

Setup: The Recruitment Brochure.indd file is open.

1. You will first view the borders of the Lab graphic itself. **Select the Direct Selection tool.**

2. **Click the Lab picture.** The picture is much wider than, but not as tall as, the frame that surrounds it.

3. **Select the Selection tool, then click the Lab picture.** The border surrounding the picture disappears, and the frame border is selected. You will now center the graphic within its frame.

4. **Choose Object→Fitting→Center Content.** The picture moves down and to the left in the frame.

5. You will now fit the picture to fill the frame. **Choose Object→Fitting→Fit Content To Frame.** The picture fills the entire frame. However, because the frame is much taller and narrower proportionally than the picture, the image is stretched vertically. You can fit the picture proportionally, which fits one dimension exactly to the frame while leaving the original image proportions intact.

6. **Choose Object→Fitting→Fit Content Proportionally.** The picture remains the same width as when you fit it to exactly fill the frame. However, it is now the correct height instead of being distorted.

7. Lastly, you will fit the frame to the current size of the content. In this case, it will shrink the height of the frame to match that of the picture. **Right-click the picture, and from the shortcut menu, select Fitting→Fit Frame To Content.** The frame's bottom edge aligns with the picture's. You will move the picture into place later.

8. You will resize the Classroom image you placed earlier. **Type 6 in the Page field at the bottom of the window and press Enter.** You are now viewing page six. You will move the picture from the pasteboard to the bottom left margin on the left page.

9. **Drag the Classroom picture so its bottom left corner snaps to the intersection of the bottom and left margins on the page.** The picture is slightly wider than the column. You will make it narrower. You will first drag a frame handle with the Selection tool to crop the picture.

10. **Drag the right center frame handle to the left until it snaps to the right column guide of the first column.** Unfortunately, part of the woman at the right side of the picture was cut off by the crop.

11. **Choose Edit→Undo Resize.** The frame returns to its original size. You will resize the picture with the frame.

12. **Hold down Ctrl, then drag the handle directly to the margin guide.**

13. **Release the mouse button, then Ctrl.** This time as you dragged, the picture was resized with the frame.

14. You will preview the graphic while resizing it. **Hold down Ctrl, hold down the mouse button on the top-right frame handle for a few moments, then drag the handle directly to the left about ½ inch.** By waiting before dragging, you enabled the dynamic graphics preview as you dragged. The picture was distorted as you dragged.

15. **Choose Edit→Undo Resize twice** to return the picture to its original size.

16. You will keep the picture proportional as you drag. **Hold down Ctrl+Shift.** Although you could drag the right middle handle again, you wish to keep the bottom edge aligned with the bottom margin. If you dragged the middle right handle, the bottom edge of the frame would move up as the frame shrunk proportionally. However, if you drag the top-right corner, the opposite corner will stay in place.

17. While still holding down the keys, **hold down the mouse button on the top-right frame handle for a moment, then drag it to the left until the right edge snaps to the right column guide.** As you dragged, the picture's proportions were maintained, so the top edge moved down as the right edge moved to the left. The picture was resized, so the woman at the right was not partially cropped as before. The picture is now the correct size and shape.

18. **Save the file.**

Topic 7B

Text Wrap

InDesign allows you great flexibility in the way text wraps around page elements. When a frame holding text is overlapped by another frame, you have several choices:

- Let the text ignore the other frame, so that it appears either in front or behind the frame.

- Wrap the text around the other frame on all sides.

- Wrap the text around the shape of the content, such as around a circular shape or the contours of a picture.

- Wrap the text above and below but not beside the frame.

- Jump the text to the next column following the frame.

You already know how to specify a text wrap to control how text wraps when one text frame overlaps another. You can use the same wrap options to control how text wraps when a graphic frame overlaps a text frame. You can control the text wrap around a frame by selecting it with either the Selection tool or the Direct Selection tool, then specifying options in the Text Wrap palette. You should select the frame that you want text to wrap around, not the frame containing the text.

TASK 7B-1

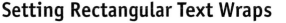

Setting Rectangular Text Wraps

Objective: To make text jump over rectangular frames.

Setup: The Recruitment Brochure.indd file is open.

1. **Navigate to page 2.**

2. If necessary, **select the Selection tool.** Currently, the picture of the student studying covers some text at the bottom of the left column, so you will make the text wrap around it.

3. **Click the picture of the student.** At first glance, you may not notice that the picture is covering any text, since no part of any characters may be visible at the top edge. However, you can tell that some text is covered, because the text at the top of the second column does not make sense following the text in the left column.

4. **Read the text in the paragraphs just before and after the picture.** The text does not make sense, because some is covered by the picture. You will fix this problem with a text wrap.

5. **Choose Window→Type & Tables→Text Wrap.** The Text Wrap palette appears.

6. You will make the text above the picture wrap jump it and continue in the next column. **Click the Jump To Next Column icon, which is the last icon.** Although the text in the column above does not change, the following text does, because it moved from beneath the picture to the top of the second column.

7. You will specify a top offset for the text wrap. **Type *p6* in the Top Offset field in the Text Wrap palette, then press Enter.** A text wrap border appears 6 points above the top edge of the picture, and it pushes the preceding text up. Since one fewer line fit in the left column, more text moved to the right column.

8. **Drag the picture straight up approximately one inch while keeping it in the left column, and release the mouse button.** Although there is enough room to fit text below the picture, the text wrap does not allow it. You will move the picture back to the bottom of the column.

9. **Drag the picture down to its original location with the bottom edge snapped to the bottom margin.** The text re-wraps. You will now create text wraps on other pages.

10. If necessary, **scroll to the right to view page three.** You will create the same type of text wrap around the picture of the students in the laboratory. This time, you will move the picture to the top of the column, and will make the text wrap below it.

11. **Drag the laboratory picture so its top edge aligns with the horizontal guide at 9p6.**

12. **Click the Jump Object icon, which is the fourth icon in the Text Wrap palette.** The text reflows below the picture. You will move the following text down away from the picture.

13. **Type *p6* in the Bottom Offset field in the Text Wrap palette, then press Enter.** The text wrap border appears 6 points below the bottom edge of the picture, and the text flows beneath it.

14. **Navigate to page 6.** You will make text flow above and below the classroom picture in the left column.

15. **Click the picture of the classroom.**

16. **Click the Jump Object icon in the Text Wrap palette.** The text reflows around the picture.

17. In the Top Offset field, **type *p6*.**

18. **Type *p6* in the Bottom Offset field, then press Enter.** The text wrap border appears above and below the edges of the picture, and the text flows around it. You will move the picture up so the Career Choices heading appears below it.

19. **Drag the picture up into the right column so the top wrap border is just below the line of text preceding Career Choices.** When you release the mouse button, the Career Choices paragraph wraps to below the picture.

We take great measures to ensure that each North Atlantic student's experience is a success story. Our curriculum and faculty will help get you where you want to go in life.

Research Opportunities

NAU is a public research university. What that means to you is that the author of your textbook may be teaching you directly. Our faculty doesn't just teach—they do. They create new technologies, initiate medical breakthroughs, discover ways to improve the environment. Whatever your major, North Atlantic faculty has experts on board to take your knowledge and experience farther than you can imagine.

Be a Big Fish

Unlike at many large schools, you won't get lost in the mix at North Atlantic. We're a big school with a small-school atmosphere. We keep the student to faculty ratio below 10/1 so you can get individualized attention. ¾ of our undergraduate courses have 35 or fewer students. Two thirds have fewer than 20, so you'll feel like you're attending

a much smaller school—while reaping the benefits of attending a well-funded research university.

Career Choices

Opportunities abound for North Atlantic graduates. Choose from the diverse following areas of concentration:

- ▸ Agriculture and Natural Resources
- ▸ Architecture
- ▸ Arts and Humanities
- ▸ Behavioral and Social Sciences
- ▸ Business and Management
- ▸ Computer, Math, and Physical Sciences
- ▸ Education
- ▸ Engineering
- ▸ Health and Human Performance
- ▸ Journalism
- ▸ Life Sciences

6

20. **Save the file.**

Irregular Text Wraps

InDesign also offers great flexibility in running text around irregularly shaped images. To wrap text around an irregularly shaped object, select the object, and in the Text Wrap palette, select the Wrap Around Object Shape icon. A text wrap border will then appear around the outside of the picture, with default outsets of 10 points.

TASK 7B-2

Creating Irregular Text Wraps

Objective: To make text wrap around non-rectangular contours or images.

Setup: The Recruitment Brochure.indd file is open.

1. You will wrap text around the basketball player image on the pasteboard of page four. **Navigate to page 4.**

2. If necessary, **scroll to the left to view the basketball player picture on the pasteboard to the left of page four.**

3. You can now set the text wrap for the picture. **Click the picture of the basketball player.** Unlike with the prior text wraps, you wish for the text to wrap around the uneven contour of the basketball backboard, rim, and the player's body.

4. **Click the Wrap Around Object Shape icon, which is the third icon in the Text Wrap palette.** A text wrap border appears around the outside of the picture, with default outsets of 10 points (written as 0p10).

5. You will have InDesign automatically detect the edges of the image and wrap around it. From the Type drop-down list, **choose Detect Edges.** The text wrap border tightly wraps around the image. You can now move the basketball player onto the page.

You can customize the wrap by dragging the handles where desired. In addition, if an image has a path applied to it in Photoshop, you can choose to wrap along that path.

If you wish for the text in a particular frame to not wrap around a frame that has a text wrap option applied, click the text frame, choose Text Frame Options from the Object menu, and check the Ignore Text Wrap check box.

6. Using the Selection tool, **drag the image onto the page so it forces the text to wrap around it approximately as shown in the following graphic. If necessary, drag the football player picture out of the way on the pasteboard.**

7. Although the text wraps to the text wrap border you created, some of the white space in the image itself covers the text that overlaps the picture's frame. You can remedy this problem by moving the picture to the back. If necessary, **click the picture of the basketball player using the Selection tool.**

8. Choose Object→Arrange→Send to Back. By moving the frame to the back, it no longer covers the text. However, the text still conforms to the text wrap border, creating the effect you desire. The text wrap is complete.

If you wish to drag the graphic frame to make the text wrap differently, you should position the mouse pointer just inside the top left corner of the frame before dragging. Otherwise, you may select the text frame that overlaps the picture.

9. Save the file.

Apply Your Knowledge 7-1

Suggested Time:

10 minutes

Placing Graphics and Applying Text Wraps

You will apply some of the skills you learned in this lesson to place another image and set two text wraps.

1.   Go to page four of the Recruitment Brochure.indd document.

2.   Create a rectangle frame at the bottom of the left column on page four that extends across the column and aligns with the bottom margin.

3.   Either drag the top handle or use the Transform palette to make it exactly 8 picas tall. Hint: Click a bottom proxy button before typing an H value in the Transform palette.

4.   Set a Jump Object text wrap, and set the top offset to p6.

5.   Place the Conversation.jpg graphic in the frame.

6. Apply a 0.5 pt black stroke to the frame.

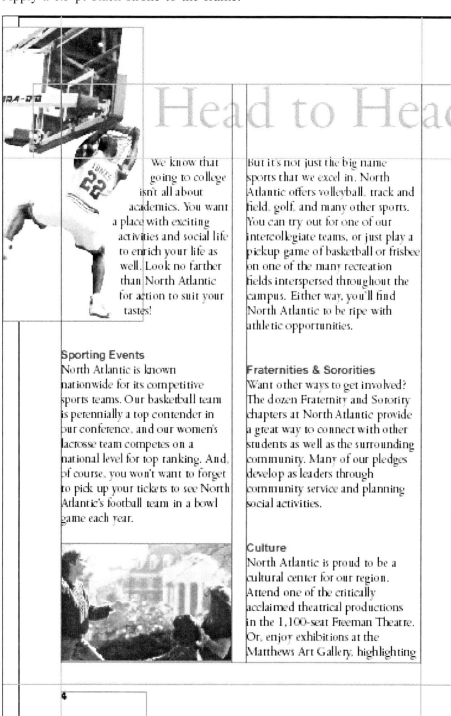

Head to Head

We know that going to college isn't all about academics. You want a place with exciting activities and social life to enrich your life as well. Look no farther than North Atlantic for action to suit your tastes!

But it's not just the big name sports that we excel in. North Atlantic offers volleyball, track and field, golf, and many other sports. You can try out for one of our intercollegiate teams, or just play a pickup game of basketball or frisbee on one of the many recreation fields interspersed throughout the campus. Either way, you'll find North Atlantic to be ripe with athletic opportunities.

Sporting Events
North Atlantic is known nationwide for its competitive sports teams. Our basketball team is perennially a top contender in our conference, and our women's lacrosse team competes on a national level for top ranking. And, of course, you won't want to forget to pick up your tickets to see North Atlantic's football team in a bowl game each year.

Fraternities & Sororities
Want other ways to get involved? The dozen Fraternity and Sorority chapters at North Atlantic provide a great way to connect with other students as well as the surrounding community. Many of our pledges develop as leaders through community service and planning social activities.

Culture
North Atlantic is proud to be a cultural center for our region. Attend one of the critically acclaimed theatrical productions in the 1,100-seat Freeman Theatre. Or, enjoy exhibitions at the Matthews Art Gallery, highlighting

7. Apply a Wrap Around Object Shape text wrap to the picture of the football player on the pasteboard to the left of page four using Detect Edges.

8. Use the Selection tool to drag the player to the bottom right corner of page five and send the graphic to the back so the text wraps approximately as shown here:

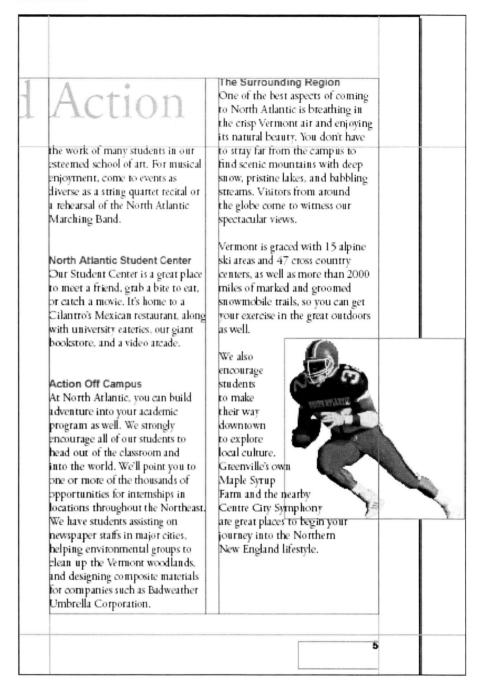

The Surrounding Region
One of the best aspects of coming to North Atlantic is breathing in the crisp Vermont air and enjoying its natural beauty. You don't have to stray far from the campus to find scenic mountains with deep snow, pristine lakes, and babbling streams. Visitors from around the globe come to witness our spectacular views.

Vermont is graced with 15 alpine ski areas and 47 cross country centers, as well as more than 2000 miles of marked and groomed snowmobile trails, so you can get your exercise in the great outdoors as well.

We also encourage students to make their way downtown to explore local culture. Greenville's own Maple Syrup Farm and the nearby Centre City Symphony are great places to begin your journey into the Northern New England lifestyle.

the work of many students in our esteemed school of art. For musical enjoyment, come to events as diverse as a string quartet recital or a rehearsal of the North Atlantic Marching Band.

North Atlantic Student Center
Our Student Center is a great place to meet a friend, grab a bite to eat, or catch a movie. It's home to a Cilantro's Mexican restaurant, along with university eateries, our giant bookstore, and a video arcade.

Action Off Campus
At North Atlantic, you can build adventure into your academic program as well. We strongly encourage all of our students to head out of the classroom and into the world. We'll point you to one or more of the thousands of opportunities for internships in locations throughout the Northeast. We have students assisting on newspaper staffs in major cities, helping environmental groups to clean up the Vermont woodlands, and designing composite materials for companies such as Badweather Umbrella Corporation.

5

9. Save the Recruitment Brochure.indd file.

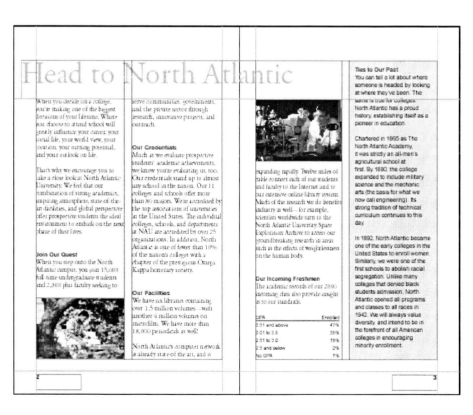

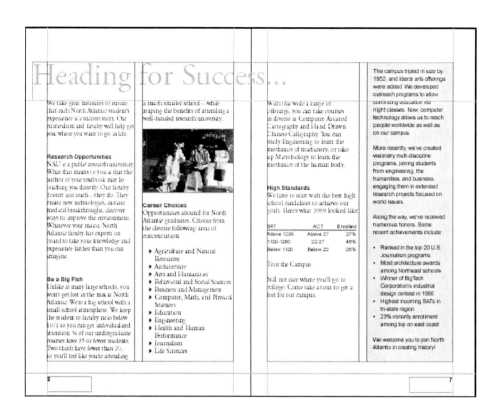

10. Close the brochure.

Topic 7C

Layers

As you've worked with InDesign, you've learned that you can place an unlimited number of items on the page. In this topic, you'll use layers to help control a page that's filled with many overlapping elements.

When you look at well-designed publications, you'll frequently find many overlapping graphic and text elements. For example, text may appear over a photograph or illustration, or images may partially cover one another. The more complex your design, the more difficult it is to select and manipulate what you want without accidentally changing something else. You can alleviate this frustrating problem by using layers, which allow you to selectively hide or lock items so they temporarily can't be viewed or edited.

You can think of layers as though they were sheets of transparency film on an overhead projector. You can see through each sheet to the ones below, and you can remove one transparency sheet to hide all of its items while still viewing the other sheets.

For a document containing text and images, you may wish to make a layer to hold the images, placed in a lower layer than the text so the text is always visible above the graphics. You could then hide the images temporarily to make it easier to edit text that overlaps them, or could lock the images layer to prevent accidentally moving them.

You could also use layers to assist in creating a multi-lingual publication, with the text in each language on a separate layer. This would enable you to make design changes to one document instead of maintaining a separate document for each language. When the document is complete, you would simply hide the layers for all but one language, then print for each language.

Creating Layers and Setting Options

To create a new layer and set options for it:

1. Choose Window→Layers to view the Layers palette.
2. Click the New Layer button or choose New Layer from the Layers palette drop-down list.
3. Double-click the layer name to access the Layer Options dialog box.
4. Type a name for the layer in the Name field.
5. Select a color for the layer that affects the color of the selection handles of items in the layer.
6. Check or uncheck Show Layer and/or Show Guides to show or hide the layer and/or guides within.
7. Check or uncheck Lock Layer and/or Lock guides to lock or unlock the layer and/or guides within.
8. Click OK to create the layer. You can double-click a layer to rename it or change any of its settings.
9. Click in a layer's Visibility column to hide it, or in its Lock column to lock it.

If you hold down Alt and click the New Layer button, InDesign will open the New Layer dialog box rather than just creating a new layer with the default settings (visible, unlocked, and named according to the order in which it was created).

Placing Items in Layers

You can place items in a layer using one of these methods:

- Click a layer name prior to creating an object; that layer will be the active layer into which new items appear.

- Select one or more items that you wish to move to another layer, and drag the dot representing selected items to another layer. If the layer you drag to is locked, a dialog box will appear asking you if you want to unlock the layer.

- Select one or more items that you wish to move to another layer, choose Edit→Cut, click another layer, and choose Edit→Paste In Place. Don't just use Edit→Paste, because that would allow the item to shift position as you paste it.

Stacking Order and Deleting Layers

To change the stacking order of layers, drag one layer up or down in the Layers palette until a black bar with triangles at the ends appears between layers in the position you wish to put the layer you're dragging.

You can delete layers either by selecting them and clicking the Delete Layer icon in the Layers palette, or by dragging them to the Delete Layer icon. If the layer contains items, a warning dialog box will appear, asking if you really want to delete the layer. You can hold down Shift and click several layers to select them simultaneously.

TASK 7C-1

Creating and Manipulating Layers

Objective: To add and manipulate layers.

1. You'll now work on a color advertisement for Fast Track Wheels, a company that manufactures bicycles, skateboards, and inline skates. **Choose File→Open, and open the Magazine Ad.indd file, located inside the Ad folder.**

2. The more you work with the magazine ad, the more you find it inconvenient to have all of the graphics and text visible and editable at all times. For example, you have found that you can easily accidentally move the large background image, and that it sometimes makes it a bit difficult to read the overlying text. To remedy these problems, you'll place the graphics on a separate layer, adjusting the layer and item stacking order as necessary. You will then lock the graphics layer to prevent movement and hide it to temporarily make text editing easier.

   You'll begin by adding a layer called Graphics to the document. **Choose Window→Layers.** The Layers palette appears.

3. **Hold down Alt and click the New Layer button at the bottom of the Layers palette.** The New Layer dialog box appears.

4. **Type *Graphics* in the Name field and click OK.** A new Graphics layer appears in the Layers palette.

If you hold down Alt as you drag a selection dot in the Layers palette, the selected items will be copied, not moved.

In many Adobe applications, including InDesign, the keyboard shortcuts for the Arrange submenu commands are Ctrl+[and Ctrl+] for moving forward or backward in the stacking order, and Ctrl+Shift+[and Ctrl+Shift+] for moving to the front or back.

5. You'll now add the images and logo to the Graphics layer. Using the Selection tool, **click the picture of the biker.** Selection handles appear around it.

6. **Hold down Shift and click the Fast Track Wheels logo, the skateboard image, and the inline skate image.** All four images are selected. The dot to the right of the Layer 1 layer represents the selected items.

7. In the Layers palette, **drag the dot on the right side of the Layer 1 layer up to the Graphics layer.** The graphics move to the Graphics layer, and now cover the type on the page.

8. You'll now position the Graphics layer below the Layer 1 layer, and try to uncover the photographs at the bottom by sending the black rectangle to the back. **Drag the Graphics layer below the Layer 1 layer in the Layers palette until a black horizontal bar appears below Layer 1.** The items on the Graphics layer are now behind those on the Layer 1 layer.

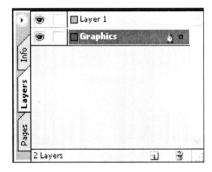

9. The black rectangle at the bottom of the page should be behind the skateboard and inline skate photographs. You'll see that you can't position it there with a stacking order command, since they're in different layers. **Click near the top left corner of the black rectangle at the bottom of the page, then try to choose Object→Arrange→Send to Back.** The menu command is grayed out, because the black rectangle is already at the back of its layer. It still covers the photographs, which are in the layer below.

10. To fix the problem, you'll move the black rectangle to the Graphics layer, then send it backwards as necessary to uncover the photographs. In the Layers palette, **drag the dot on the right side of the Layer 1 layer down to the Graphics layer.** The black rectangle moves to the Graphics layer. Since it came from a layer that was above this one, it remains at the top of the stacking order within the Graphics layer.

11. **Choose Object→Arrange→Send Backward twice** to uncover both the skateboard and inline skate images.

12. You'll lock the Graphics layer to prevent yourself from accidentally moving any of its items. In the Layers palette, **click in the Lock column to the left of the Graphics layer.** An icon of a pencil with a slash through it appears.

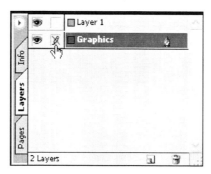

13. **Try to drag the image of the biker.** The image stays in place because the layer is locked.

14. Hiding the Graphics layer can make it easier to read text that overlaps darker parts of the background photograph, such as the top of the second column. In the Layers palette, **click in the Visibility column to the left of the Graphics layer.** The eye icon disappears in the palette, and the graphics disappear on the document page. The body text is now easier to read.

15. Using the Type tool, **double-click the word toughest at the top of the second column of body text.**

16. **Type** *most rugged,* to replace it.

17. In the Layers palette, **click in the Visibility column to the left of the Graphics layer.** The eye icon reappears in the palette, and the graphics reappear on the document page. The body text you edited partially covers a dark part of the image, and was easier to see with the Graphics layer hidden.

18. This advertisement has been scheduled to run in European magazines as well as American ones, so it needs to be produced in multiple languages. You'll add a French version of the text without having to use a separate document by putting the text on a different layer. **Create a new layer called French Text.**

19. **Hide the Layer 1 layer.** The English text disappears.

20. You'll bring the French text in from another document. **Open the French Ad Copy.indd file in the Ad folder in the 078195Data folder.**

21. The type on this page is in the same position as it is in the English version; you'll simply copy and paste it in place in the French Text layer. **Choose Edit→Select All, then choose Edit→Copy.**

22. You can now close the French document. **Close the French Ad Copy.indd document, and don't save changes if prompted.** You return to the Magazine Ad.indd document.

23. **Choose Edit→Paste In Place.** The French ad copy appears.

24. You can easily choose to edit or print either language. **Hide the French Text layer and show Layer 1.** You've returned to editing the English text. The ad is complete.

25. Save and close the file.

Summary

In this lesson you used several techniques to place and manipulate graphics. You placed graphics into new frames and existing ones, used commands to control the size and position of graphics within frames, and wrapped text around graphics.

Lesson Review

7A **Why do pictures sometimes appear jagged and blocky when imported into InDesign, and what can you do about it?**

Why might you want to create a frame before placing a picture in InDesign?

7B **How can you specify that text wrap around a graphic?**

How can you specify that text wrap around an irregular shape?

7C **Name one way to move an existing item from one layer to another.**

How can you hide a layer's contents?

Transparency

Overview

In this lesson, you'll work with InDesign's powerful transparency features. You'll apply transparency to imported images and graphics, as well as objects you create within InDesign. You will also use effects to add drop shadows and feathering. Lastly, you'll ensure that transparency prints properly by using transparency flattener presets.

Data Files
Catalog.indd

Lesson Time
15 minutes

Objectives

To create design effects using transparency, you will:

8A   **Apply transparency to objects.**

You'll control the transparency of both InDesign items and imported images.

8B   **Apply effects that require transparency.**

You'll apply drop shadows, feathering, and blending modes to InDesign elements.

8C   **Choose Transparency Flattener settings.**

You'll control how InDesign converts transparency into a single layer of artwork for printing to obtain the best balance of quality and performance.

Topic 8A

Applying Transparency

Designers apply transparency to objects in order to allow graphics or text to show through the transparent object. InDesign enables you to use a range of transparency effects.

The Transparency palette, shown in Figure 8-1, enables designers to apply a variety of transparency effects to text and graphics. All objects in an InDesign file can have transparency applied to them; including text, placed vector and bitmap graphics, and InDesign-created design elements. To adjust an object's transparency, drag the Opacity slider in the Transparency palette, or type a value in the Opacity field.

InDesign accepts native Illustrator files with transparency as well as EPS files. InDesign also accepts varying levels of opacity in Photoshop files (not just clipping paths, which only offer simple on/off transparency silhouetting).

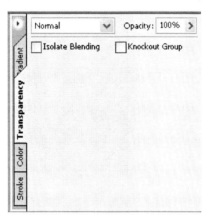

Figure 8-1: *The Transparency palette enables designers to apply a variety of transparency effects to text and graphics.*

TASK 8A-1

Using Transparent Objects

Objective: Add transparency to an object.

Setup: The files used in this task are located in the Catalog folder.

1. You will begin by opening another document, a catalog for Fast Track Sports. You will then import some objects that contain transparency, and apply transparency to an object you draw in InDesign. **Open the Catalog.indd document, which is located in the Catalog folder.**

2. **Go to page one.** At Typical Display, the logo image at the top of the page (an EPS file) is quite pixilated, although its transparency is apparent.

3. You'll improve the display of all of the images in the document to clearly view the transparency effects you create with InDesign. **Choose View→ Display Performance→High Quality Display.** The logo's onscreen appearance is much improved.

4. **Go to page 8.**

5. You'll place an Illustrator version of the logo. **Place the Fast Track Logo.ai image above the text "is a division of."**

6. You'll now place a Photoshop file. **Place the Action Play Logo.psd image beneath "is a division of."** The soft Photoshop transparency is displayed in InDesign.

7. **Place the Inline Skate.psd and Skateboard.psd images above their labels.** You have finished placing transparent objects into the document. Next you will draw a rectangle and change its transparency.

8. **Draw a 16p x 18p (WxH) rectangle that surrounds the text and images in the bottom corner of the page.**

9. **Apply a fill of Paper and a stroke of None to the rectangle.**

10. You will change its fill to be somewhat transparent so you can see the image behind it. **Click the Transparency palette tab.**

11. With the rectangle selected, **drag the Opacity slider to approximately 60%.**

12. **Choose Object→Arrange→Sent To Back, then Object→Arrange→Bring Forward** to move the rectangle behind the other images except for the background photo.

13. **Position the rectangle as shown in the following graphic.**

 **Topic 8B**

Transparency Effects and Blending Modes

Along with simple opacity controls and importing images with transparency, InDesign allows you to use transparency for creative effects. Choosing Object→ Drop Shadow applies a semi-transparent drop shadow to any object, and choosing Object→Feather blends the edges of an object gradually into its background. Both of these effects are dynamic—if the item or text to which they're applied changes, the shadow or feathering changes instantly. When applying transparency or a drop shadow or feather effect to text, select the text using the Selection tool. You can't apply these effects to text selected with the Type tool.

You can also select from the following transparency blending modes, which control how the colors of a foreground item interact with those of background items. For example, a foreground item in Multiply mode will always appear darker than it would in Normal mode because its colors combine with those of the items behind it almost like overlaying two colored transparencies on an overhead projector. As with any aspect of InDesign transparency, you can apply these modes to any item, including images that already contain transparency effects from Illustrator or Photoshop. You can specify a blending mode from the Transparency palette's Blending Mode drop-down list.

Blending Mode	Description
Normal	The default transparency mode, colors the selection with the blend color, without modifying with the base color.
Multiply	Creates a darker color by multiplying the base color by the blend color.
Screen	Creates a lighter color by multiplying the inverse of the blend and base colors.
Overlay	Depending on the base color, multiplies or screens the colors. Preserves the highlights and shadows of the base color while mixing in the blend color.
Soft Light	Depending on the blend color, darkens or lightens the colors. The effect is like shining a soft spotlight on the image.
Hard Light	Depending on the base color, multiplies or screens the colors. The effect is like shining a harsh spotlight on the image.
Color Dodge	Brightens the base color so that it reflects the blend color.
Color Burn	Darkens the base color so that it reflects the blend color.

Blending Mode	Description
Darken	Uses the darker of the base or blend colors to determine the resulting color.
Lighten	Uses the lighter of the base or blend colors to determine the resulting color.
Difference	Depending on whether the base or blend color has a greater brightness value, subtracts the blend color from the base color, or the base from the blend, to determine the resulting color.
Exclusion	Creates a low contrast version of the Difference blending mode.
Hue	Results in an output color with the luminance and saturation of the base color and the hue of the blend color.
Saturation	Results in an output color with the luminance and hue of the base color and the saturation of the blend color.

Blending Mode	Description
Color	Results in an output color with the luminance of the base color and the hue and saturation of the blend color.
Luminosity	Results in an output color with the hue and saturation of the base color and the luminance of the blend color.

TASK 8B-1

Applying Transparency Effects

Objective: To apply transparency effects.

Setup: The Catalog.indd file is open.

1. You will apply a 1p6 diffuse feather to the rectangle. This will make the rectangle appear to fade out at the edges. With the rectangle selected, **choose Object→Feather.** The Feather dialog box appears.

2. **Check the Feather check box.**

3. You can change the feather width. In the Feather Width field, **type *1p6.***

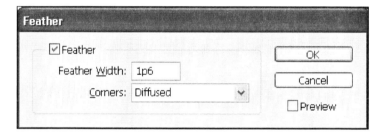

4. **Click OK.**

5. You will apply a drop shadow to the text and the inline skate and skateboard images. **Click the words "is a division of."**

6. **Hold down Shift and click "Be sure to check out...," "Inline Skates," "Skateboards," and the pictures of the inline skate and skateboard.** All of those items are selected at the same time.

7. **Choose Object→Drop Shadow.** The Drop Shadow dialog box appears.

8. **Check the Drop Shadow check box.**

9. You can choose the shadow's size and position. In the X Offset field, **type *0p2.***

10. In the Y Offset field, **type *0p2.***

11. In the Blur field, **type *0p2.***

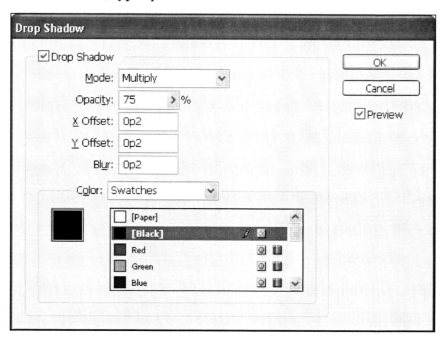

12. **Click OK.** The text and images all have drop shadows applied.

13. **Change the word "division" to "subsidiary" with the Type tool.** The drop shadow changes to reflect the new wording.

14. You'll apply a blending mode to the Fast Track Wheels logo to darken it so it has more contrast against the light background. **Click the Fast Track Wheels logo with the Selection tool.**

15. In the Transparency palette, **choose Multiply from the Blending Mode drop-down list.** The logo darkens slightly.

16. The transparency effects are complete. **Save the file.**

Topic 8C

Printing with Transparency

When your document contains transparency, InDesign uses flattening to merge the artwork in a document into a single printable layer. Flattening is a technology that blends overlapping objects that have transparency applied to them into one flat set of opaque objects. It is featured in Adobe Illustrator, as well as in InDesign.

During flattening, InDesign finds areas where transparent objects overlap other objects, and divides the objects into components as shown in Figure 8-2.

| Original | Objects divided into components |

Figure 8-2: *InDesign flattens images containing transparency, dividing overlapping objects into separate components.*

InDesign gives you the tools to control how your documents are flattened. InDesign's flattener feature maintains *vectors* as vectors, whenever possible, to increase print speed and for higher quality output. However, as necessary, vectors are converted to *rasters*. In addition, when you print or export to EPS or PDF, the document's transparency may be retained in the output, which means that it is fully editable.

InDesign's Edit→Transparency Flattener Presets command enables you to select and customize the settings that you use to flatten a document. In addition, InDesign provides the capability to save, export, and import transparency flattener presets so multiple people can use the same settings for consistent, reliable output. You can also control the flattening for individual spreads by choosing Spread Flattening from the Pages palette drop-down list.

The following table describes the transparency flattening parameters in the Transparency Flattener Presets dialog box:

Transparency Flattener Parameter	Description
Raster/Vector Balance	Determines whether objects with transparency are rasterized upon output or maintained as vector objects. When the slider is set closer to the Vectors end, less rasterization will be performed on the file's graphics. This is somewhat dependent on the complexity of the file and the variety of objects included in the transparency flattening.
Line Art and Text Resolution	Sets the resolution of objects that are rasterized when the file is flattened. This setting should correlate with the output resolution.

Transparency Flattener Parameter	Description
Gradient and Mesh Resolution	Controls the resolution of gradients within rasterized objects. Gradients are also transparency effects, such as feathering, drop shadows, etc. In most cases, a setting of 300 dpi will provide sufficient resolution.
Convert All Text to Outlines	Ensures that when transparent text objects are flattened, the width of text characters remains consistent.
Convert All Strokes to Outlines	Maintains stroke width consistency between stroke objects that contain transparency and those that do not.
Clip Complex Regions	Eliminates color stitching, which results when the rasterization of complex graphics causes pixels to be rendered in a blocked or stitched fashion.

Regardless of the flattener settings, it's wise to avoid applying numerous transparency effects, particularly overlapping ones, to many pages in a document; excessive use of transparency can slow down performance in InDesign and during printing. You can preview the areas in your document that will be affected by transparency flattening using the Flattener Preview palette. To open the palette, choose Window→Output Preview→Flattener. In the Flattener Preview palette's Highlight drop-down list, select the category of items you want to preview. The items described by that category that are affected by transparency flattening will then appear with a red highlight.

If your default printer is a PostScript printer, you can choose one of the flattener presets from the Preset drop-down list in the Transparency Flattener section. If the default printer isn't PostScript, you can't control InDesign's transparency flattening at print time. Most consumer inkjet printers aren't PostScript.

TASK 8C-1

Applying Transparency Flattener Presets

Objective: To preview InDesign's transparency flattener presets.

Setup: The Catalog.indd file is open.

1. **Select Edit→Transparency Flattener Presets.** The Transparency Flattener Presets dialog box appears.

2. **Click the Low Resolution, Medium Resolution, and High Resolution presets.** Line art and text items that InDesign's flattener needs to rasterize will print at 288 pixels per inch (ppi) with the Low Resolution setting, 300 ppi with the Medium Resolution, and 1200 ppi at High Resolution.

3. You won't edit these settings now, but you will choose one to apply when you print to a PostScript printer. **Click OK.**

4. You will choose from one of the transparency flattener presets when you print. **Choose File→Print.** The Print dialog box appears.

5. **Click Advanced in the category list on the left.**

6. You won't print now, so you'll cancel the Print dialog box. **Click Cancel** to close the dialog box.

7. **Save and close the Catalog.indd document.**

Summary

You've seen how InDesign's transparency features allow for great design creativity, enabling you to apply effects to any item and to make anything semi-opaque. InDesign also allows precise control over printing transparent items so you can get the best balance of quality and performance.

Lesson Review

8A To which objects can you apply transparency effects in InDesign?

How can you adjust an item's transparency in InDesign?

8B How can you apply a dynamic drop-shadow effect to text?

What do blending modes control?

8C Briefly explain what flattening does.

How can you quickly identify items in a document that will be affected by transparency flattening?

YOUR NOTES:

Using Tables

Overview

You may often need to include tabular data in your layouts. Previously, you used tabs to organize data. In this lesson, you'll create tables that integrate smoothly with other page content.

Data Files
Catalog.indd

Lesson Time
30 minutes

Objectives

To add tables to a document, you will:

9A   Create a table.

You will convert tabbed text to a table.

9B   Format tables.

You will format table cells to make them easier to read and more attractive.

Topic 9A

Creating Tables

When you have information that you need organized in columns and rows, you should consider creating it as a table rather than simply typing it as text in a text block. You can create a table by creating a text frame, and with the insertion point flashing within the text frame, choosing Table→Insert Table. In the Insert Table dialog box, you can then specify the number of columns and rows, as well as the number of header and footer rows. Header and footer rows are useful for a table that may be split across multiple threaded text frames, because they repeat at the top or bottom of the portion of the table that appears within each threaded text frame. After creating the table, you can place the insertion point within a table cell, and type to add text. You can press Tab to move the insertion point to the next cell. When you reach the last cell in the table's body, pressing Tab again creates an additional body row.

You can also convert existing paragraphs of text into a table so that tab, comma, or paragraph break characters in the text indicate where new columns and rows occur. To convert text to a table, select the text using the Type tool, then choose Table→Convert Text To Table. In the Convert Text To Table dialog box, specify the characters in the text that should indicate where new columns and rows occur.

Table Modifications

After creating a table, you may want to modify the table. The columns are initially the same width. Using the Type tool, you can position the mouse pointer on the right edge of a column so that it appears as a double arrow, then drag to the right to widen the column, or to the left to make it narrower. Likewise, you can position the mouse pointer on the bottom edge of a row, then drag down or up to increase or decrease the row height. In addition, you can select multiple columns whose widths don't match, and choose Table→Distribute Columns Evenly so that the columns' widths are evenly divided over the existing combined width of the selected columns. You can similarly distribute multiple rows to use the same height by selecting the rows, then choosing Table→Distribute Rows Evenly.

You can adjust the row height or column width by selecting the rows or columns you want to modify, then choosing Table→Cell Options→Rows And Columns. In addition, you can adjust the vertical alignment of a cell's contents, as well as an inset for the cell's contents, by choosing Table→Cell Options→Text.

To select a column, select the Type tool, then position the mouse pointer in the top of the column you want to select so that it appears as a down-pointing arrow, and click. You could also position the mouse pointer in the top of a column and drag to the left or right to select multiple columns. In the same way, you can position the mouse pointer at the left edge of a row to select one or more rows. To select one or more adjacent cells within the table, position the mouse pointer within the first cell you want to select, and drag to select additional cells. You can also select rows, columns, or the entire table using commands from the Table→Select submenu or from the shortcut menu that appears when you right-click within the table.

You can merge cells together by selecting the cells to merge, and choosing Table→Merge Cells. If you later decide to unmerge the cells, you can choose Table→Unmerge Cells. However, if each cell contained text or graphics before being merged, the contents of the unmerged cells may now appear together in one of the cells, rather than in their original cells. In that case, if the Undo command is available, you should choose it to unmerge the cells, rather than use the Unmerge Cells command.

TASK 9A-1

Converting Text to Tables

Objective: To convert text to a table.

Setup: You will use the Catalog.indd file.

1. **Open the Catalog.indd document and browse through the document to view each spread of pages.** As you can see, there are three areas with unformatted tabbed text that needs to be formatted as a table.

2. **Go to page four.**

3. **Use the Type tool to select all the tabbed text on the bottom section of page four and zoom in to 150%. Select the text from "Small" to the sentence that begins, "See page seven..." at the bottom.**

4. You will now convert this text to a table. **Choose Table→Convert Text to Table.** The Convert Text To Table dialog box appears.

5. From the Column Separator drop-down list, **select Tab, and in the Row Separator drop-down list, select Paragraph.**

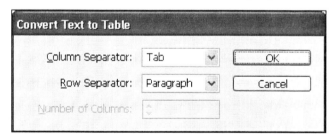

Click OK.

6. At this point, each column is the same width. However, you would like the first column to be wider then the others, since it contains longer text. You will widen the first column, then evenly distribute the remaining space between the other columns. **Position the mouse pointer on the right side of the first column.** The mouse pointer changes to a double arrow.

7. Drag to the right until the first column is wide enough to display each item on one line.

	Small	Medium	Large
Frame Size	38	43	48
Frame Weight	See disclaimer on page seven		
Head Angle	71°	71°	71°
Seat Angle	73°	73°	73°
Top Tube Length	57	60	62
Rider Height	<5'6"	5'5"-6'1"	>5'10
Stand Over Height	67	71	75
Head Tube Length	9	11	13
Chain Stay Length	42	42	42
BB Height	34	34	34
Wheel Base	107	107	107
BB Width	73mm	73mm	73mm
Seat Post Size	27.2mm	27.2mm	27.2mm
Headset Size	1.125"	1.125"	1.125"
All measurements in cm unless otherwise designated.			

8. When you widened the first column, the table also increased in size. **Position the mouse pointer on the right edge of the table, and drag to the left until it reaches the right margin.**

9. Now you will change the three columns to be the same width. **Position the mouse pointer in the top of the second column, and drag to the right to select the last three columns.**

	Small	Medium	Large
Frame Size	38	43	48
Frame Weight	See disclaimer on page seven		
Head Angle	71°	71°	71°
Seat Angle	73°	73°	73°
Top Tube Length	57	60	62
Rider Height	<5'6"	5'5"-6'1"	>5'10
Stand Over Height	67	71	75
Head Tube Length	9	11	13
Chain Stay Length	42	42	42
BB Height	34	34	34
Wheel Base	107	107	107
BB Width	73mm	73mm	73mm
Seat Post Size	27.2mm	27.2mm	27.2mm
Headset Size	1.125"	1.125"	1.125"
All measurements in cm unless otherwise designated.			

10. **Choose Table→Distribute Columns Evenly.** The three columns are all now the same width.

11. Finally, you will merge three cells. You would like the cell with the text see disclaimer to spread across three columns. **Select the three cells in the Frame Weight row.**

	Small	Medium	Large
Frame Size	38	43	48
Frame Weight	See disclaimer on page seven		
Head Angle	71°	71°	71°
Seat Angle	73°	73°	73°

12. **Choose Table→Merge Cells.**

	Small	Medium	Large
Frame Size	38	43	48
Frame Weight	See disclaimer on page seven		
Head Angle	71°	71°	71°
Seat Angle	73°	73°	73°
Top Tube Length	57	60	62
Rider Height	<5'6"	5'5"-6'1"	>5'10
Stand Over Height	67	71	75
Head Tube Length	9	11	13
Chain Stay Length	42	42	42
BB Height	34	34	34
Wheel Base	107	107	107
BB Width	73mm	73mm	73mm
Seat Post Size	27.2mm	27.2mm	27.2mm
Headset Size	1.125'	1.125"	1.125"
All measurements in cm unless otherwise designated.			

13. **Select the four cells in the last visible row, then choose Table→Merge Cells.** An additional row that was overset should now be visible at the bottom of the table.

14. Merge the cells in the final row.

	Small	Medium	Large
Frame Size	38	43	48
Frame Weight	See disclaimer on page seven		
Head Angle	71°	71°	71°
Seat Angle	73°	73°	73°
Top Tube Length	57	60	62
Rider Height	<5'6"	5'5"-6'1"	>5'10
Stand Over Height	67	71	75
Head Tube Length	9	11	13
Chain Stay Length	42	42	42
BB Height	34	34	34
Wheel Base	107	107	107
BB Width	73mm	73mm	73mm
Seat Post Size	27.2mm	27.2mm	27.2mm
Headset Size	1.125"	1.125"	1.125"
All measurements in cm unless otherwise designated.			
See page seven for notes.			

15. Save the file.

Importing a Table from Word

If you import a Word or RTF document that includes rows assigned as heading rows, the heading rows are converted to header rows within InDesign.

If you have a table that exists in Microsoft Word or Excel, you can place it into an InDesign document, and it will contain its formatting. To place a table, choose File→Place, select the file containing the table, and click Open. A loaded text icon appears, which you can click to place the imported table. Once you've imported a table, you can modify it just like any other table.

TASK 9A-2

Importing a Table

> **Objective:** To import a table from a Microsoft Word document.
>
> **Setup:** The Catalog.indd file is open.

1. Choose Edit→Deselect All.

2. You will import a table into page five. **Go to page 5 and choose File→ Place.** The Place dialog box appears.

3. Select the Hybrid Table.doc document, and click Open. The mouse pointer changes to show that you are importing text.

4. Click below the image of the bike to place the table. The table appears on the page.

5. You will change the width of the last three columns. **Position the mouse pointer on the right edge of the table, and drag to the left until you reach the right margin.**

6. Now you will change the three columns to be the same width. **Position the mouse pointer in the top of the second column, and drag to the right to select the last three columns.**

7. **Choose Table→Distribute Columns Evenly.** The three columns are all now the same width.

8. You will also increase the row height of the cells and center the text vertically. **Choose Table→Select→Table** to select the entire table.

9. **Choose Table→Cell Options→Rows and Columns.** The Cell Options dialog box appears.

10. In the Row Height field, **type *1p2*.**

11. **Click the Text tab.**

12. **Choose Center from the Align drop-down list, then click OK.**

13. **Save the file.**

Topic 9B

Formatting Tables

Once you've added raw data to a table, you'll format it. Just as formatting text makes it more appealing to look at and easier to read, text formatting is an important part of creating tables. Left unformatted, a table can look like a sea of numbers, and can be difficult to scan quickly for information. When you apply formatting, the table becomes more useful, and can match the look of the document into which it's placed as well.

Applying formatting to type in a table is the same as it is anywhere else in InDesign. You can apply all of the typographic effects you've learned. You can apply formatting to the text in multiple table cells at once.

You can also apply formatting to the table cells, columns, and rows themselves. Once you select a table cell, row, or column, you can apply fill and stroke attributes using the same techniques you use to apply fills and strokes to other objects. After selecting a table, cell, row, or column, you can apply a color to the text in the selected cells by first selecting the Formatting Affects Text option. You can also choose Table→Table Options→Alternating Fills to fill alternating rows with a color.

TASK 9B-1

Applying Formatting to Tables

Objective: To format tables.

Setup: The Catalog.indd file is open.

1. **Go to page four.**

2. You will begin by changing the top row of the table to white text on a black background. **Click in the first row, and choose Table→Select→Row to select the first row.**

3. **Specify a black fill using the Color palette.** The selected cells are filled with black.

4. **Click the Formatting Affects Text icon in the Color palette.**

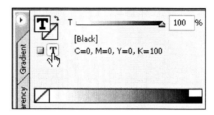

5. **Choose the white color swatch in the Color palette. Click elsewhere in the table to deselect the first row.** The top row now has white text on a black background.

6. You want to alternate a white row with a gray row. **Choose Table→Select→ Table to select the entire table.**

7. **Choose Table→Table Options→Alternating Fills.** The Table Options dialog box appears.

8. From the Alternating Pattern drop-down list, **choose Every Other Row.**

You may need to apply the color twice if it does not remain the first time you apply it.

9. You will have the fill skip the first two rows, since you already formatted the first row yourself with a black fill. In the Skip First field, **type 2.** You will keep the default setting of grey and white alternating fills.

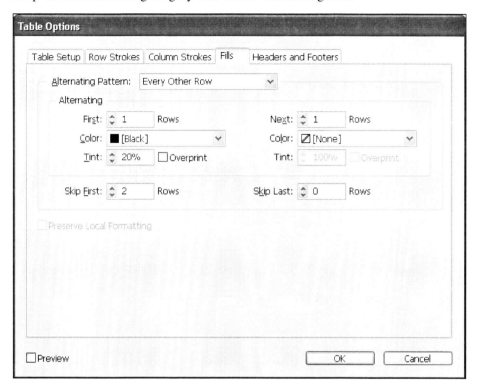

10. Click OK.

	Small	Medium	Large
Frame Size	38	43	48
Frame Weight	See disclaimer on page seven		
Head Angle	71°	71°	71°
Seat Angle	73°	73°	73°
Top Tube Length	57	60	62
Rider Height	<5'6"	5'6"-6'1"	>6'10
Stand Over Height	67	71	75
Head Tube Length	9	11	13
Chain Stay Length	42	42	42
BB Height	34	34	34
Wheel Base	107	107	107
BB Width	73mm	73mm	73mm
Seat Post Size	27.2mm	27.2mm	27.2mm
Headset Size	1.125"	1.125"	1.125"
All measurements in cm unless otherwise designated			
See page seven for notes.			

11. You would like to add a blue fill to the note at the bottom of the table. You can drag a swatch to a table cell to format it. **Drag the blue swatch from the Swatches palette to the bottom cell.** The bottom cell is now filled with a light tint of the blue color.

12. Save the file.

Apply Your Knowledge 9-1

Now that you have learned how to create and format tables, you will practice what you have learned by adding another table to the document.

1. Convert the tabbed text on page six to a table.

2. Change column width and merge cells as you did in the table on page four.

3. Format the table similar to the one on page four.

4. If the bottom row is not visible, use the Selection tool to move the whole table up a bit, then drag the bottom handle down to make more room.

	Small	Medium	Large
Frame Size Center-Top	52	57	63
Frame Weight	See disclaimer on page seven		
Head Angle 2	72°	73°	74°
Seat Angle 2	75°	74°	73°
Top Tube Length	53.5	57	63
Rider Height 3	5'3"-5'7"	5'7"-6'2"	>6'2"
Stand Over Height 4	77	81	87
Head Tube Length	10.5	14	20
Chain Stay Length	41	41	41
BB Height 2	27.5	27.5	27.5
Wheel Base	95	99	104
BB Width	70mm	70mm	70mm
Seat Post Size	26.8mm	26.8mm	26.8mm
Headset Size	1.125"	1.125"	1.125"
All measurements in cm unless otherwise designated.			
See page seven for notes.			

5. Save and close the document.

Summary

In this lesson, you created, modified, and formatted tables. Tables are an effective way to present data that is easy to read and understand.

Lesson Review

9A How do you create an empty table?

How do you convert text into a table?

9B How can you format text within a table?

How can you apply a color to table cells?

YOUR NOTES:

Preparing for Handoff to a Service Provider

LESSON

10

Data Files
*Magazine Ad Complete.
indd*

Lesson Time
30 minutes

Overview

The commercial printing process is somewhat more complex than desktop printing, and it involves carefully transferring all of the necessary files to the printer in formats that won't cause production problems. In this lesson, you'll describe commercial printing, and will preflight and package a document to ensure that it will print properly the first time when you send it out.

Objectives

To send documents out to commercial printers reliably, you will:

10A **Understand the commercial printing process.**

You'll examine how a document is traditionally printed on a press, with color separations that divide the document into ink components.

10B **Use the Links palette and Preflight command to search for potential problems in InDesign documents.**

You'll ensure that the image you view in InDesign is the most recent version, and will use the Preflight command to run the document through a comprehensive test for problems.

10C **Proof a document on a desktop printer.**

You will choose appropriate print settings for printing an InDesign document.

10D **Package files for commercial printing.**

You'll package the files necessary for printing in one folder to send to a printing company.

 Topic 10A

Commercial Printing Overview

Before sending documents to a commercial printer, you should familiarize yourself with several color printing concepts.

Color printing is produced by using one or more color inks. Depending on the complexity of the document, you may use as few as one, or as many as six or more inks. If the pages contain full color photographs, the document must be printed with at least four inks: the colors cyan, magenta, yellow, and black (CMYK), also known as process color or four-color printing.

Desktop Printing

Desktop color printers all use these four colors in the form of inks, dyes, toner, or waxy crayon-like sticks, to reproduce all printed colors. Some desktop color printers use additional inks to allow for a broader range, or gamut, of colors, but all use at least the CMYK colors. This course will refer to desktop color printers, and any other printers that create color output directly to a page (such as color copiers), as composite printers, because they combine all of the inks directly onto the finished medium at once. Composite printers are usually used for low print quantities, and as proofs for publications that will be commercially printed.

Commercial Printing

If you need to produce a large number of color pages, it is inefficient to use a composite printer. Instead, your document can be printed on a press. This section briefly describes the process of preparing documents for printing to press. This process is known as prepress.

imagesetter:
An output device that generates high-resolution output from a computer file, typically for camera-ready content.

Instead of printing directly to a page, you prepare color separations for the press. Each color separation is a grayscale representation of where one color ink is to be applied to the page. Color separations are typically printed from the computer, passing through a Raster Image Processor (RIP) to an _imagesetter_, which outputs to film instead of paper. Light is then shone through the film to expose a photosensitive material, which is used to create a printing plate. The printing plate is then mounted to the press, and rollers transfer the image from the plate to the paper.

Figure 10-1 shows the appearance of the film separations for a typical process color page. Note the black text appearing only on the black plate, and how combining two or more inks forms other colors. For example, the block at the bottom of the page is red, and appears on the magenta and yellow plates.

Color Page

Cyan Plate   Magenta Plate   Yellow Plate   Black Plate

Figure 10-1: *Process color separations.*

Most printing companies in the United States print a negative image to film, unlike printing to paper. These negative prints are basically the same as negatives you may have received with your photographs when you've had your camera's film processed. On a negative print, the areas where ink is to be applied are transparent, and the areas that are to remain the color of the paper are black, which is the original color of the film. This method prevents dirt or fingerprints on the majority of the film from appearing on the printing plate and the final printed piece.

Spot Color Separations

Another advantage to printing color separations, as opposed to composite color printing, is that you can add spot colors to the page. Spot colors are printed with one pre-mixed ink instead of combining the four process color inks. They are typically chosen from an ink manufacturer's swatchbook, such as the PANTONE Matching System. Spot colors allow you to use a specific color, that won't vary, when a specific color is important. For example, spot colors are sometimes used for a logo.

Spot colors are frequently used to save on printing costs; one-, two-, or three-ink printing jobs are less expensive than process color jobs, which use four inks. As an example, many two-ink publications combine a spot color with black, or use two spot colors.

If you are already printing with CMYK inks, it may not be necessary to use spot color, since a wide variety of colors are already available to you. If your document did not contain any CMYK images, you could reduce costs by using three or fewer spot colors, including black.

However, there are times when it is necessary to combine process and spot colors on a printed page. Since process color printing has a relatively small range of printable colors, or gamut, many bright, vibrant colors are impossible to achieve using CMYK. However, you can choose spot color inks from a much broader gamut. Additionally, pre-mixed spot color inks are more likely to match the intended color than colors mixed from process inks on press, so they are frequently used for company logos and other instances when color matching is critical. Spot colors can also be used for specialty purposes, such as for metallic inks or varnish plates.

Figure 10-2 shows a page with spot color in the title (the letters nips in the word Snips) printed with a spot color. The word only appears on the spot color plate, so would be printed with a PANTONE(r) ink instead of a combination of cyan, magenta, yellow, and black.

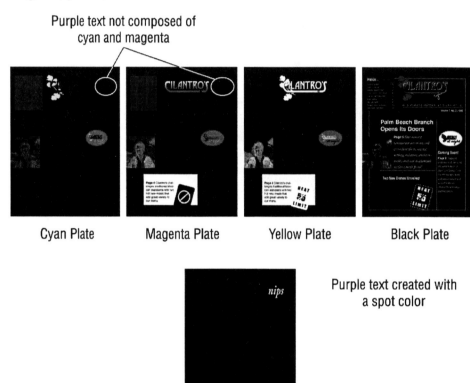

Figure 10-2: *Process color separation with one spot color.*

TASK 10A-1

Commercial Printing

1. **What type of printing combines all of the inks directly onto the finished medium at once and is usually used for low print quantities?**

2. **What is the advantage to using a spot color?**

Topic 10B

Preflighting

To search for potential problems in InDesign documents, you can use preflighting. Preflighting involves the use of the Links palette and the Preflight command.

The Links Palette

When you place a picture into an InDesign document, it does not ordinarily add all of the image data to the document. Instead, InDesign notes the location of the original image file on the hard disk, and refers to it when you print. This approach of linking to the original image file on the hard disk keeps the InDesign document size small, but requires InDesign to keep track of all of the files you have placed. If InDesign cannot find a picture file when you print the document, the low-resolution preview image will be printed instead, creating unacceptable results.

You can use the Links palette to control a document's links.

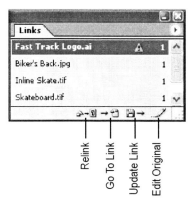

Figure 10-3: *The Links palette, showing a document with three functioning links and one problem.*

You can click a link's name, and click one of the following buttons at the bottom of the palette:

Button	Purpose
Relink	Click to locate a file if the original has been moved so InDesign can't find it.
Go to Link	Jump to the page and zoom in on a linked image or text in the document.
Update Link	Redraw the page onscreen to reflect the most recent version of the linked document.
Edit Original	Open the linked document in the application that created it. For example, open a vector EPS file in Illustrator or a TIFF file in Photoshop.

TASK 10B-1

Updating Linked Images

Objective: To update linked images.

1. In this lesson, you'll work with a version of the Fast Track Wheels advertisement that is almost ready to send for commercial printing, but needs to be checked for problems. **Open the Magazine Ad Complete.indd file in the Ad for Print folder within the 078195Data folder.**

2. InDesign displays a dialog box warning you that one of the links in the document has been modified. Although you could click Fix Links Automatically to let InDesign try to remedy the problem on its own, you'll see how you can do so manually with the Links palette, which you may need at times when InDesign can't simply fix the problem. **Click Don't Fix.**

3. If necessary, **choose Window→Links.** The Links palette appears, listing all of the placed files in the document.

4. The Fast Track Logo.ai file has an exclamation point beside it, indicating that something is wrong with it. **Position the mouse pointer over the exclamation point and wait a moment for the Tool Tip to appear.** InDesign indicates that this file has been modified since the time it was placed. This means that the image's appearance in the document doesn't reflect how it will really print, since the current version of the image file will be used for printing.

5. You'll fix this problem by updating the link. Before updating, **note the color of the Fast Track Wheels logo at the bottom of the document.** The logo was originally white when it was placed in this document, but was since changed in Illustrator.

6. If necessary, **click Fast Track Logo.ai in the Links palette.**

7. **Click the Update Link button in the Links palette.** After a moment, the page redraws and a gradient appears on the logo characters.

8. The links are now all up to date. **Save the document.**

The Preflight Command

InDesign offers a powerful utility command for checking your document for problems. While it can't find every potential mistake, it can alert you to issues you wouldn't have otherwise noticed. It checks for fonts, links and images, colors and inks, and print settings. To preflight a document, choose File→Preflight. InDesign then takes a few moments to check the fonts, links, images, colors, inks, and print settings, and then the Preflight dialog box appears. You can select from categories on the left side of the dialog box to view document details about specific document components.

The summary category will summarize the document's preflight information, indicating whether there are identified problems in a particular category.

The Fonts category lists all the fonts used in the document. Even if no problems are listed, you should always check to ensure that only the fonts you intended to use are listed.

The Links And Images category lists all the images used in the document, along with their link status and other details. It may indicate that there is a problem with a particular image, even when the image is linked properly, if the image was saved in the RGB color space. This would prevent the image from being color separated if color management is not turned on. Even with color management active, this acts as a warning to indicate that the image's printed colors may shift significantly from its appearance onscreen, since the RGB color space has a much different gamut than that of CMYK.

The Colors And Inks panel indicates the inks, angles and halftone screen frequencies, which are measured in lines per inch. If the total number of inks exceeds the number of inks that can be used by the press you will print on, you should reduce the number of inks. Otherwise, the document will have to be passed through the press more than once, greatly increasing the cost of the job.

The Print Settings category reflects the settings saved with the document. These settings are only saved when you print the document. Some, but not all, can be saved ahead of time. Therefore, this panel has limited usefulness for checking print settings before printing—some will likely be incorrect until after the job has been printed at least once.

Once you have checked for and corrected any problems listed in the Preflight dialog box, you can click the Report button to create a report that you can give to a printing company. Additionally, you can click the Package button to package all of the files necessary for printing in one folder for convenience.

In addition to preflighting for printing problems, you should also usually check for misspellings by choosing Edit→Check Spelling. InDesign allows you to add words to multiple dictionaries, so you can create your own customized list of words specific to different circumstances.

TASK 10B-2

Preflighting Documents and Packaging for Printing

Objective: To check your document for errors and prepare it for sending to a commercial printer.

Setup: The Magazine Ad Complete.indd file is open.

1. **Choose File→Preflight.** After a few moments, the Preflight dialog box appears.

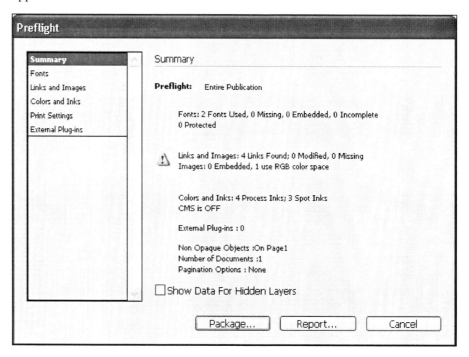

2. The summary page indicates that there is a problem with the links and images, since one of the images was saved in the RGB color space. You will examine each category in detail. **Click Fonts in the category list on the left side of the dialog box.** The Fonts panel appears.

3. If necessary, **uncheck the Show Problems Only check box.** The list of all fonts used in the document appears. Only Verdana Regular and Verdana Bold were used, so the fonts are as you expect.

4. **Click Links And Images in the category list on the left side of the dialog box.** The Links And Images panel appears.

5. Since you already examined the links with the Links palette, you will look only at what the Preflight dialog box considers to be problems. If necessary, **check the Show Problems Only check box.** The only problem is the RGB file. You will change it in a moment by relinking to another image.

6. **Click Colors And Inks in the category list on the left side of the dialog box.** The Colors And Inks panel appears. The total of seven inks is too high for the press you will print on, so in a moment, you will limit the inks to six so you can print in one pass.

7. **Click Print Settings in the category list on the left side of the dialog box.** The Print Settings panel appears.

8. You should return to the document to fix the problems before proceeding. **Click Cancel.**

9. You should now eliminate one spot color. The color Blue should be a process color, so you'll convert it to the CMYK color mode to reduce the number of inks to six. You should deselect all objects before using the Swatches palette to avoid coloring anything. **Choose Edit→Deselect All.** All objects are deselected.

10. **Double-click the Blue swatch in the Swatches palette.** The Swatch Options dialog box appears.

11. **Choose Process from the Color Type drop-down list, then click OK.** The color Blue will now print using cyan and magenta inks instead of as a spot color.

12. You'll use the Links palette to relink the RGB Biker's Back.jpg image to a CMYK version that the art department converted in Photoshop. In the Links palette, **click Biker's Back.jpg.**

13. **Click the Relink button.** The Locate File dialog box appears.

14. **Double-click the Biker's Back CMYK.jpg file in the Ad for Print folder.** The image is relinked to the CMYK version.

15. You've made all of the changes necessary to print the document reliably. **Save the file.**

Topic 10C

Printing

Now that you have profligate the advertisement, you will print a proof to ensure that it prints as you intend it. If a document doesn't print properly for you, it likely won't print correctly for a commercial printer.

InDesign's Print dialog box is efficiently organized to make choosing options straightforward, as shown in Figure 10-4.

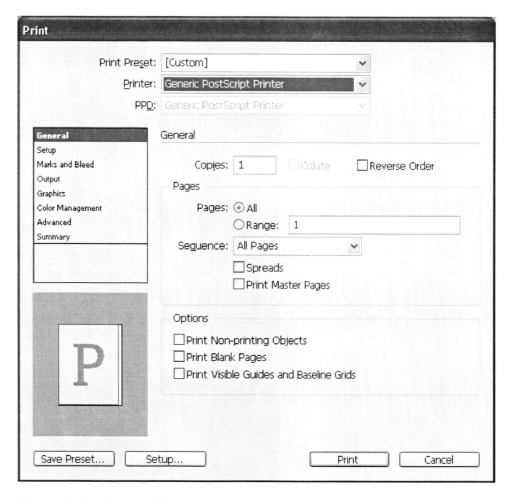

Figure 10-4: *InDesign's Print dialog box is efficiently organized to make choosing options straightforward.*

The Print dialog box is divided into eight setting categories.

You can use the Separations Preview palette to view overprint preview, multiple color plates, single plates, and ink limits in a document. To open the palette, choose Window→Output Preview→ Separations.

- General settings allow you to control the number of copies, pages and sequence, and useful options for designers such as the ability to print master pages, visible guides and baseline grids, and non-printing objects and blank pages.

- Setup settings control the paper size and orientation, scaling, position of the image on the page, as well as options for printing *thumbnails* and *tiling*.

- Marks & Bleeds settings allow you to add printers marks and control how much of the pasteboard surrounding each page should be printed. You can set the bleed distance at each edge separately.

thumbnails:
Several reduced-size pages printed per sheet of paper.

- Output settings let you choose to create a composite or color separations. When printing separations, you can control prepress settings such as trapping, screening, and inks.

- Graphics settings let you control how images and fonts are sent to the printer, and let you choose the PostScript level and data format.

tiling:
A large document page printed across several sheets of paper.

- Color Management settings allow you to achieve accurate color matches between the document as it appears on screen and printers. Color management works by determining the color reproduction characteristics (the color space) of each device you use (for example, your monitor and printer), and writing the information about each in a profile. When you enable color management by choosing Edit→Color Settings, you can designate which color profiles for RGB and CMYK colors are applicable to the document. InDesign accepts color management profiles embedded in placed images and graphics, so it can adjust the color of Photoshop and Illustrator images that were prepared in different color spaces than the one you're viewing. The Color Management Policies section of the Color Settings dialog box lets you control how to handle such profile mismatches. When you print, InDesign can translate the colors from the document (source) color space to the printer's color space (again, as saved in a color profile).

- Advanced settings let you specify OPI image replacement settings, substituting low-resolution proxy images for the high-resolution ones for working in InDesign and reducing network traffic, but printing the high-resolution versions. You can also how InDesign handles gradients and transparency.

- Summary settings include a list of all of the settings you chose in the other categories, and allows you to save the information in a text file that you can keep for future reference or pass along to a printing vendor.

TASK 10C-1

Printing the Document

> **Objective:** To print a document to a desktop printer.
>
> **Setup:** The Magazine Ad Complete.indd file is open.

1. Since this document's page size is larger than 8½″ x 11″, it ordinarily wouldn't fit on letter size paper. However, you can choose to scale the document down for printing to your printer if you don't have one that can print larger pages. **Choose File→Print.** The Print dialog box appears.

2. You will not change most of the settings from the defaults, but will scale the page to fit on the paper. **Click Setup in the category list on the left side of the dialog box.**

3. **Select the Scale To Fit option.** The document scales as necessary to fit on the paper chosen in the Paper Size drop-down list above.

4. If you have a physical printer attached, **click Print. Otherwise, click Cancel.**

Topic 10D

Packaging Files

You can use the Preflight dialog box to create a report and to package the files for printing. While you can choose File→Package to create the package, it's a good idea to use the Package button within the Preflight dialog box to ensure that there are no last-minute problems. You can package the files into a new folder, ensuring that the printing company gets all the necessary files without any unnecessary files, along with a report for the modified file and its links.

When packaging files, you can specify several options in the Package Publication dialog box.

- The Copy Fonts (Roman Only) check box allows you to specify whether to include copies of the font files for all fonts used in the document.

- The Copy Linked Graphics check box allows you to specify whether to include copies of all linked graphics used in the document.

- The Update Graphic Links In Package check box allows you to specify whether the graphic links are updated in the copy of the InDesign file moved to the package folder, based on the new location of the files within that folder.

- The Use Document Hyphenation Exceptions Only check box allows you to specify whether hyphenation exceptions specified within the InDesign application will impact your file. InDesign can save rules indicating how specific words are to be hyphenated both on the computer and within individual InDesign documents. To keep the hyphenation exceptions stored on a printing provider's computer from affecting your document, you should only allow the hyphenation exceptions stored in the document to take effect.

- The Include Fonts And Links From Hidden Layers check box allows you to specify whether to include fonts and links on hidden layers.

- The View Report check box allows you to specify whether to view the report that is generated, which contains the information from the Printing Instructions dialog box, as well as detailed information on fonts, colors and inks, links and images, print settings, and a file package list. The report is generated, whether or not you check this check box. This check box simply allows you to specify whether to view the report automatically once it's generated.

- The Instructions button allows you to specify printing instructions for the print shop.

TASK 10D-1

Packaging Files for Handoff

Objective: To package the files needed for commercial printing.

Setup: The Magazine Ad Complete.indd file is open.

1. **Choose File→Preflight.** The Preflight dialog box appears after InDesign checks the document.

2. There are now only six inks and no RGB images, so the document is ready to be sent to the printer.

   You will opt to package the files for printing. **Click Package.**

3. The Printing Instructions dialog box appears. If you wished, you could fill out this information in full to give to the printing company responsible for outputting the publication. You will use the default for now (the filename refers to the report name, not the newsletter's name). **Click Continue.**

4. The Package Publication dialog box appears. You will place the package of files on the Desktop where it is easy to find. From the Save In drop-down list at the top of the dialog box, **choose Desktop.**

5. You will keep the ad's filename the same as it was. You will include fonts and linked graphics. If necessary, **check the Copy Fonts (Roman Only) and Copy Linked Graphics check boxes.**

6. Since InDesign will create an entire new folder with a copy of each of the files, you should update the links so the InDesign file links to the graphics in the package folder. **Check the Update Graphic Links in Package check box.**

7. You don't want the hyphenation exceptions stored on the printing provider's computer to affect your document. **Check the Use Document Hyphenation Exceptions Only check box.**

8. You will view the report InDesign creates. **Check the View Report check box.**

9. You can now create the package of files for printing the Catalog. **Click Package.**

10. InDesign issues an alert warning you to not violate the font foundry's license agreement by giving fonts to unauthorized people. **Click OK.**

11. InDesign gathers all of the files into a folder on the Desktop. It also creates the report, which it opens in a text editor application. **Scroll through the report.**

12. **Choose File→Exit.** The document closes and the text editor quits.

13. You will examine the package folder on the desktop. **Close any Windows Explorer/My Computer windows and hide any applications as necessary to see the Magazine Ad Complete Folder folder on the desktop.**

14. **Double-click the Magazine Ad Complete Folder folder on the desktop.**
The InDesign document, instructions text file, fonts, and links are neatly packaged.

15. **Return to InDesign.** InDesign appears. The open document is the original version in the InDesign CS Publishing Data folder on your hard disk, not the one you just packaged.

16. **Save and close the file.**

Summary

In this lesson you described the commercial printing process and profligate a document to ensure that it will print properly when you send it out to a print vendor.

Lesson Review

10A What is the main difference between desktop color printing and commercial printing?

In terms of the available colors you can print, what is an advantage of commercial printing, as opposed to desktop printing?

10B Why is it important to maintain the links to placed graphics in your publication?

Name two problems that may be present in your document that the Preflight dialog box does not report as problems.

10C How do you ensure that a large page will fit on the paper to which you're printing?

How do you add printers marks to a document when you print it?

10D What elements does the Package command gather for handoff to a commercial printer?

When packaging files to send to a commercial printer, how can you include the fonts with the files you package?

Creating Acrobat PDF Files

Overview

The Acrobat PDF (Portable Document Format) file format provides a versatile way of distributing files. Since any computer on any platform can read PDF files with the free Adobe Reader application (formerly known as Acrobat Reader), or with the full Adobe Acrobat application, they are commonly used on the World Wide Web to issue information in documents that need to be formatted for convenient printing. They are also used for passing files to commercial printing companies, because their file sizes are usually much smaller and often easier to print than original document files or PostScript files. When you use PDF to send a job to a print provider, you don't have to worry about including linked files or fonts, because they're embedded in the single PDF file. In this lesson, you will create Adobe Acrobat PDF files.

Data Files
Recruitment Brochure. indd

Lesson Time
30 minutes

Objectives

To create PDF files for different purposes, you will:

11A **Choose settings for PDF files intended for the Web.**

You'll create a small document that can be downloaded as quickly as possible, and is reasonable quality for viewing on screen.

11B **Create PDF presets.**

You'll save the settings from the PDF Export settings dialog box as presets, which facilitate changing many settings with one menu choice.

11C **Choose settings for PDF files intended for commercial printing.**

You'll focus on ensuring high-quality results for publications intended for printing on a press. The file size will be larger than that of the PDF for the Web, but the images will appear crisper and clearer.

Topic 11A

PDF Files for the Web

The primary objective when producing a PDF file for distribution via the Internet is small file size. Although high-quality appearance is somewhat important, you will generally choose options that reduce the size at the expense of image resolution and sharpness. In addition, when generating a PDF file that will be viewed onscreen, you can add bookmarks as a document navigation aid.

Bookmarks

Before exporting an InDesign file to PDF, you can specify bookmarks for the exported PDF file using the Bookmarks palette. A bookmark is a text entry that appears in the Bookmarks panel within Acrobat or Adobe Reader, which users can click to navigate to a predetermined location within the PDF document. Bookmarks are often created to correspond to each section of a document. The Bookmarks panel within Acrobat then becomes a sort of table of contents for your file, as shown in Figure 11-1, and those viewing the file can click a specific bookmark to navigate directly to the section they want to view.

Figure 11-1: *Bookmarks can be designed as a sort of table of contents for navigating a file within Acrobat or Adobe Reader.*

To open the Bookmarks palette, choose Window→Interactive→Bookmarks. To generate bookmarks for specific elements within the file, select text or another item you want to add as a bookmark in the PDF file, then in the Bookmarks palette, click the New Bookmark button. If the bookmark is based on selected text, its name will match the selected text. The name will be highlighted so you can type to change it, if desired. When you generate the PDF file, bookmarks will be generated for the elements you specified. After creating a bookmark, you can select from the Bookmarks palette drop-down list to rename or delete a selected bookmark, or to navigate to the bookmark's destination within the document.

If you create a table of contents using Layout→ Table Of Contents, then in the Table Of Contents dialog box, check the Create PDF Bookmarks check box so that the table of contents entries automatically generate bookmarks when the file is exported to PDF.

You can also create a bookmark by selecting text or another item, then right-clicking it and from the shortcut menu, and selecting Interactive→New Bookmark.

If you want to add a bookmark that appears as a "child" indented below a "parent" bookmark, then first select the bookmark in the Bookmarks palette that should act as the parent. Then select the text or item you want to use as a child bookmark, and click the New Bookmark button.

You can also specify hyperlinks within an InDesign file you're exporting to PDF. Hyperlinks are composed of sources — the object or text that you click — and destinations — the location (a URL or document page) that is displayed when the source is clicked. You can use the Hyperlinks palette (Window→Interactive→Hyperlinks) to create new hyperlinks, control the display of the source, and define hyperlink destinations.

TASK 11A-1

Specifying Bookmarks

Objective: To specify bookmarks for a file when exported to PDF.

Setup: You will use the Recruitment Brochure.indd file.

1. **Open the Recruitment Brochure.indd file, located within the Brochure folder.**

2. You want to generate a bookmark for each of the main sections. **Navigate to page 2, and use the Type tool to select the page heading, Head to North Atlantic!**

3. **Choose Window→Interactive→Bookmarks.** The Bookmarks palette appears.

4. **Click the New Bookmark button, then press Enter.**

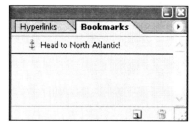

5. **Navigate to page 4, and add a bookmark for the page heading, Head to Head Action.**

6. **Add a bookmark for the page heading on page 6, Heading for Success.**

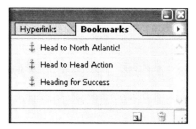

7. You will now add the subheadings in each main section so that they'll appear indented below each of their respective parent bookmarks. In the Bookmarks palette, **select the Head to North Atlantic! bookmark.**

8. On page 2, **select the heading, Join Our Quest, then click the New Bookmark button. Press Enter.** The bookmark appears indented below the parent bookmark, Head to North Atlantic.

9. **Add the remaining headings as bookmarks so that each one appears indented below the parent bookmark to which it belongs.**

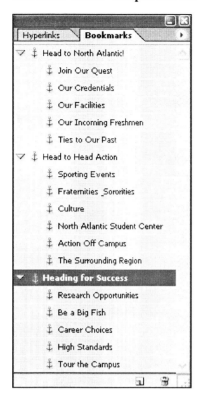

10. **Save the file.** When you export the file to PDF in the next section, the bookmarks will be generated in the PDF file.

PDF Export Settings for Web

To save a PDF copy of an InDesign file, choose File→Export, and from the Save As Type drop-down list, select Adobe PDF, then click Save. The Export PDF dialog box appears. You can enter settings within six different categories. However, you can also choose from the Preset drop-down list to quickly set all of the options at once.

To save a PDF file that will be viewed only onscreen, you can specify Screen from the Preset drop-down list. The following settings will then automatically be set:

- Bookmarks and hyperlinks you've specified in the InDesign file will be exported with the PDF file.

- Image compression for color and grayscale images will be set to 72 ppi (pixels per inch). PDF documents intended for the Web should contain low resolution graphics to keep the file size down. Although 72 ppi is far too low for high-quality printing, it is adequate for viewing on screen, since that resolution is comparable to a monitor's.

- Printers marks are turned off, and bleed values are set to 0. PDF documents intended for the Web don't need printer's marks such as crop marks and color bars for calibration. Similarly, since they're not intended for printing on oversize paper and trimming, the bleed values are all 0.

- Advanced settings are set to minimize file size and to display the file most appropriately on the Web. Since monitors are RGB devices, Web Potfuls should generally contain RGB, not CMYK images. They should usually embed the fonts used within so the viewer doesn't have to have them, but should subset them, so only the characters used in each font are included. This keeps the file size to a minimum. Web PDF files don't require Open Prepress Interface image replacement, which is typically used to lessen network traffic by substituting low-resolution images for the final high-resolution ones used for printing. Lastly, if the image contains transparency, the low resolution flattener style is sufficient.

• By default, no password is required to open, edit, or print the file. You can specify a password to open the file, or a separate password to restrict the ability to edit or print the file.

TASK 11A-2

Exporting PDF Files for Web Distribution

Objective: To create a compact PDF file for distribution via the Internet.

Setup: The Recruitment Brochure.indd file is open.

1. **Choose File→Export.** The Export dialog box appears.

2. You will save this file to the Desktop to make it easy to find. From the Save In drop-down list, **choose Desktop.**

3. It is a good idea to use all lowercase file names for the Web with a three letter extension. In the File Name field, **type *brochureweb.pdf.***

4. **Choose Adobe PDF from the Save As Type drop-down list, then click Save.** The Export PDF dialog box appears.

5. You'll create your first PDF by using one of the default styles. From the Preset drop-down list, **choose Screen.**

6. **Click General in the category list on the left side of the dialog box.** The Bookmarks check box is checked, so the bookmarks you specified will be included in the PDF file.

7. **Click Compression in the category list on the left side of the dialog box.** Color and grayscale images will be compressed to 72 ppi.

8. **Click Marks And Bleeds in the category list on the left side of the dialog box.** The printer's marks are all turned off, and the bleed values are all 0.

9. **Click Advanced in the category list on the left side of the dialog box.** These settings are set to minimize file size and to display the file most appropriately on the Web.

10. **Click Security in the category list on the left side of the dialog box.** No password will be required to open, print, or edit the file.

11. All of the settings are complete. You can now export the PDF document intended for distribution via the Internet. **Click Export.** InDesign generates the PDF file on the desktop.

12. You'll view the document you just created. **Hide InDesign and any Windows Explorer/My Computer windows so you can locate the brochureweb.pdf document on the desktop.**

13. **Right-click the brochureweb.pdf document and choose Properties from the shortcut menu that appears.** This document is between 200 and 300 k in file size, which is acceptably small for distribution via the Web.

14. **Close the Properties window.**

15. **Double-click the brochureweb.pdf document.** Your default PDF document viewer launches and opens the document.

16. You will use the generated bookmarks to navigate through the PDF file. **Choose View→Fit In Window** (or View→Fit Page).

17. **Choose View→Continuous-Facing** (or View→Page Layout→Continuous-Facing).

18. If necessary, on the left side of the screen, **click the Bookmarks tab to display the bookmarks.**

19. **Click the bookmarks to view each spread of pages.** The images are lower resolution than the originals, but are acceptable for viewing onscreen.

20. **Return to InDesign.**

Topic 11B

PDF Presets

If you need to make PDF files for more than one purpose, you may find it useful to save the settings you create in the Export PDF dialog box. InDesign lets you create PDF presets for this purpose. A PDF preset is a menu choice you name that recalls all of the Export PDF dialog box settings for a specific setup. PDF presets are saved with InDesign preferences, so they're available for printing any document. However, this flexibility means that document-specific settings, such as security settings, can't be saved in PDF presets.

The process of creating PDF presets is similar to saving printer presets. Once you've created presets, you can simply choose one to access the Export PDF dialog box with the settings already chosen. At that point, you can set document-specific settings, override any of the other settings you desire, then create the PDF file.

To create a PDF preset, choose File→PDF Export Presets→Define. In the PDF Export Presets dialog box, select an existing preset on which you want to base the new preset, then click New. In the New PDF Export Preset dialog box, specify a name for the preset. The name you enter here will appear in a menu, and will be available to all InDesign documents, not just the specific one you're working on. You can then specify the settings you want to use for the preset.

Unlike when you used the Export PDF dialog box directly, the Security settings are not available when you create a PDF preset, because those settings are document specific, and PDF presets can be used with any document. However, you can set security options when you actually export a PDF file using the PDF preset you've created.

TASK 11B-1

Creating PDF Presets

Objective: To save PDF export settings so they can be recalled later with one menu choice.

Setup: The Recruitment Brochure.indd file is open.

1. You'll now alter some settings slightly and save them in a PDF preset. **Choose File→PDF Export Presets→Define.** The PDF Export Presets dialog box appears.

2. You'll create a variation on the Screen preset, so you'll select it first. **Click Screen.**

3. **Click New.** The New PDF Export Preset dialog box appears.

4. In the Name field, **type *Web*.**

5. You'll choose to view the PDF immediately after creating it. **Check the View PDF After Exporting check box.**

6. To allow for even smaller file sizes, you'll reduce the compression quality to Low for color and grayscale images. **Click Compression in the category list on the left side of the dialog box.**

7. From the Image Quality drop-down lists under Color Images and Grayscale Images, **choose Low.**

8. The PDF preset settings are complete. **Click OK.** You return to the PDF Export Presets dialog box. You'll create another PDF preset, so you don't need to close this dialog box.

Topic 11C

PDF Files for Printing

Another purpose for PDF files is to provide them as files for printing. The PDF format is capable of high-quality printing, and even color separations. Unlike preparing files for Web distribution, PDF files intended for printing should contain high resolution, high quality images. The file size will be larger, but since the file transfer speed over a network is not the main concern, this is a good tradeoff for the increased quality.

You can select the Press preset to specify settings appropriate for high-quality commercial printing. The Print preset is more appropriate for general use printing from desktop printers. Since file size isn't a concern for PDF files intended for print, color and grayscale image resolution will be limited to 300 ppi, which is adequate for desktop printing, and even for most high-resolution color separations. You can ensure excellent quality by eliminating compression for color and grayscale images.

TASK 11C-1

Exporting PDF Files for Printing

Objective: To create a high quality PDF file for printing.

Setup: The Recruitment Brochure.indd file is open.

1. You will define a PDF preset for creating PDF files intended for desktop printing. You'll alter some of the settings saved in the Press preset. In the Presets list, **click Press.**

2. **Click New.** The New PDF Export Preset dialog box appears.

3. In the Name field, **type *Max Quality Prepress.*** The Bookmarks check box is unchecked, since this file is intended for print, rather than onscreen viewing.

4. You'll now edit the settings to save them with the style. As with the Web style you created, you wish to open the PDF file immediately after creating it. **Check the View PDF After Exporting check box.**

5. Since file size isn't a concern, color and grayscale image resolution is limited to 300 ppi, which is adequate for desktop printing, and even for most high-resolution color separations. You'll eliminate compression for color and grayscale images. **Click Compression in the category list on the left side of the dialog box.**

6. From the Compression drop-down lists under Color Images and Grayscale Images, **choose None.**

7. The PDF preset settings are complete. **Click OK.** You return to the PDF Export Presets dialog box.

8. You've finished creating PDF presets. **Click OK.**

9. You'll now try the Max Quality Prepress setting to compare the output and file size to the one you created for the Web earlier. **Choose File→Export.** The Export dialog box appears.

10. From the Save As Type drop-down list, **choose Adobe PDF.**

11. **Type *Brochure for Printing.pdf* in the File Name field, then click Save.** The Export PDF dialog box appears.

12. **Choose Max Quality Prepress from the Preset drop-down list, then click Export.** InDesign generates the PDF file and opens it immediately per your choice.

13. **Choose View→Fit In Window** (or View→Fit Page).

14. **Choose View→Continuous-Facing** (or View→Page Layout→Continuous-Facing).

15. **Press Page Down four times to view each spread of pages.** The images are much higher resolution than they were in the Web version.

16. Lastly, you'll view the Info window for the document you just created to determine its file size. **Exit your PDF viewer application, then hide InDesign and any Windows Explorer/My Computer windows** so you can locate the Brochure for Printing.pdf document on the desktop.

17. **Right-click the Brochure for Printing.pdf document and choose Properties** from the shortcut menu that appears. This document is around 6 MB in file size, which would be large for a file transfer via the Web but not a problem for printing.

18. **Close the Properties window.**

19. **Return to InDesign, and save and close all open files.**

Summary

In this lesson, you saved InDesign documents with settings that control the image quality and file size. You created a small file size with lower quality for the Web, and a higher quality file with higher file size for printing. You specified bookmarks within the generated PDF file to aid in onscreen navigation. You also saved settings for creating PDF files so you can easily select them as a group rather than individually choosing options each time.

 Lesson Review

11A How can you generate bookmarks for an InDesign file you export to PDF?

What image resolution is good for color and grayscale images in PDF documents intended for the Web?

11B Why is it useful to create PDF presets?

Which category of PDF export settings cannot be saved as part of a pre-set?

11C What image resolution is good for color and grayscale images in PDF documents intended for desktop printing?

Which PDF preset is appropriate for professional, high-quality printing?

Adobe Certified Expert (ACE) Objective Mapping

APPENDIX

A

Adobe Certified Expert (ACE) Program

The Adobe Certified Expert (ACE) Program is for graphic designers, Web designers, developers, systems integrators, value-added resellers, and business professionals who seek recognition for their expertise with specific Adobe products. Certification candidates must pass a product proficiency exam in order to become an Adobe Certified Expert.

Selected Element K courseware addresses product-specific exam objectives. The following table indicates where InDesign® CS exam objectives are covered in Element K courseware.

ACE Objectives:	InDesign® CS:	
	Creating Basic Publications (Level 1) Topics	Creating Sophisticated Type, Graphics, and Cross-Media Publishing (Level 2) Topics
1.0 General Knowledge		
1.1 List and describe key features and benefits of Adobe InDesign. (Key features include: XML support, books, page layout features, text handling).	1A	7A, 7B, 7C, 9A, 9B
1.2 List and describe the features that allow users to manage palettes (i.e., workspace management).	1A	
1.3 Explain how Adobe InDesign provides support for interoperability with other Adobe products (products include: Photoshop, Illustrator, GoLive, Acrobat).	7A, 8A, 10B, 11A, 11B, 11C	4B, 5A, 5C, 9A
2.0 Setting Up Documents		
2.1 Given a scenario, describe what is affected by selecting various settings.	2B	
2.2 Given a scenario, create a new document by using the Document Setup dialog box.	2B	
2.3 Create and apply document styles.	2A	
2.4 Given a scenario, create the structure of a document by using guides and grids.	3A	
2.5 Given a scenario, work with Master pages (scenarios include: creating, applying, basing a new Master page off an existing Master page, overriding Master page items).	3A, 3B	1A

ACE Objectives:	InDesign® CS:	
	Creating Basic Publications (Level 1) Topics	Creating Sophisticated Type, Graphics, and Cross-Media Publishing (Level 2) Topics
2.6 Create and use graphic and text placeholders and containers.	7A	
2.7 Explain how objects are organized in InDesign by using layers (options include: viewing, locking, stacking, rearranging, selecting, copying, merging, flattening).	7C	
3.0 Working with Text		
3.1 Given a scenario, format text by using the appropriate palette or menu item.	2C, 6A, 6B	
3.2 Insert special characters by using the Type menu, Glyph palette, or contextual menu.	6A	
3.3 Manipulate text by using frame options (frame options include: threading, frame properties, resizing, text wrap, selecting text).	4B, 4C, 6D	
3.4 Create, apply, import, and modify styles by using the Character Style and Paragraph Style palettes.	6C	2A, 2B, 2C
3.5 List and describe the advantages and disadvantages when using OpenType, True- Type, or Type 1 fonts.	6A	
4.0 Drawing, Arranging, and Transforming Objects		
4.1 Describe how you can create and edit paths by using the appropriate InDesign tools.		5A, 5B, 5C
4.2 Create, edit, and thread text on a path.		5C
4.3 Modify and transform objects by using various InDesign features.		5C, 5E
4.4 Modify the contents of frames by using various InDesign features.	1A, 6D, 7A	5D
5.0 Working with Color		
5.1 Create, edit, and apply colors to objects by using the appropriate palettes.	5A	
5.2 Explain when you would use the Swatches palette versus the Color palette.	5A, 5B	
5.3 Given a scenario, create, modify and apply gradients to objects by using the appropriate palettes and tools.	5B	
5.4 Explain the purpose of color management, and discuss color management workflows in Adobe InDesign.	10C	
6.0 Working with Transparency		
6.1 Given a scenario, apply transparency to an object.	8A, 8B	
6.2 Describe how Adobe InDesign supports transparency features in Placed files (file formats include: Photoshop, Illustrator).	8A, 8B	
6.3 Given a scenario, create and/or apply the proper flattening style to achieve the desired output.	8C	8B

ACE Objectives:	InDesign® CS:	
	Creating Basic Publications (Level 1) Topics	Creating Sophisticated Type, Graphics, and Cross-Media Publishing (Level 2) Topics
7.0 Importing and Exporting Files		
7.1 Select the appropriate method and file format for importing text and graphics.	4A, 7A	
7.2 Given a scenario, select the appropriate file format and options for exporting an Adobe InDesign document to PDF.	11A, 11B, 11C	
7.3 Manage Placed graphics by using the Links palette including editing the original in the source application.	10B	
8.0 Managing Long Documents		
8.1 Create a book by using the Book palette.		7C
8.2 Create a Table of Contents and Index by using the appropriate palettes and commands.		7A
8.3 Create and manage hyperlinks by using the Hyperlinks palette.		9B
8.4 Synchronize styles and swatches in a book.		7C
9.0 Preparing Documents for Cross-Media Support		
9.1 Describe workflows that are enabled by using XML.		9A
9.2 Import an XML file into an InDesign document.		9B
9.3 Define and assign XML tags, and export an XML file.		9A
9.4 Map styles to XML tags by using the Tags palette and the Structure view.		9A
9.5 Import a DTD and validate XML structure against the DTD.		9A
10.0 Working with Tables		
Create and import tables.	9A	
Modify tables.	9A	
Format a table.	9B	
11.0 Prepress and Outputting to Print		
Describe which elements are checked and flagged during the preflight process.	10B	
Describe the resulting objects when a package is prepared.	10D	
Configure print settings in the Print dialog box for various types of output.		8A, 8B

LESSON REVIEW 1

Topic 1-A

What is the area outside the pages in the document window called?

The area outside the pages is the pasteboard.

What is the difference between the Selection tool and the Direct Selection tool?

The Selection tool manipulates entire frames; for example, you can use it to move a text or graphic frame. The Direct Selection tool is used to manipulate the contents of the frame or reshape the frame's border. For example, you can use the Direct Selection tool to drag a graphic within the frame without moving the frame itself.

Topic 1-B

What keyboard shortcut can you press to access the Zoom tool without using the Toolbox?

Press Ctrl+Spacebar to access the Zoom tool; press Ctrl+Alt+Spacebar to access the Zoom Out mouse pointer.

List at least two techniques for navigating among InDesign document pages.

Answers include:
- *Scroll using the Hand tool or scrollbars.*
- *Use the Page controls at the screen's bottom left.*
- *Use the Pages palette.*
- *Use the Layout menu's page navigation commands.*

LESSON REVIEW 2

Topic 2-A

How do you type values in inches when the default measurement system is set to picas?

Type i or an inch mark (") after the value to designate inches.

How can you create a new document and specify its document settings?

Choose File→New→Document, and in the New Document dialog box, specify settings.

Topic 2-B

What do X and Y represent in the Transform palette?

The X value is the distance from the 0 mark on the horizontal ruler to the point selected in the proxy. The Y value is the distance from the 0 mark on the vertical ruler to the point selected in the proxy.

Why are there no buttons for applying type styles such as bold and italic in InDesign?

Some fonts were not intended by the designer to be boldfaced or italicized, so only those type styles that the font is designed to use are available.

Topic 2-C

Which tool (Selection tool or Direct Selection tool) do you use to crop an image?

You use the Selection tool to crop an image; dragging a frame handle with the Direct Selection tool distorts the frame.

How can you import a graphic into an InDesign document?

Choose File→Place, select the file you want to place, then click Open. Position the mouse pointer where you want to place the graphic, then click to place the graphic.

LESSON REVIEW 3

Topic 3-A

What is the main purpose of creating masters?

Masters can hold items that should appear on several pages in the document.

What is the difference between dragging a horizontal ruler guide to the page or to the pasteboard?

Ruler guides dragged to a page appear only on that page; ruler guides dragged to the pasteboard span both pages.

Topic 3-B

How can you type into a text frame that appears on a document page but that was created on a master?

Hold down Ctrl+Shift and click the frame to convert it from a master frame to a document frame, then edit the text in the frame as usual.

How can you apply a master to a document page using the Pages palette?

- *Drag the master icon onto the document page icon.*

- *Drag the master's name onto the document page icon.*

- *Select one or more document page icons, then from the palette's drop-down list, select Apply Master To Pages.*

LESSON REVIEW 4

Topic 4-A

How can you import text into an InDesign document?

To place text, choose File→Place, then select the file you want to place and click Open. Click the loaded text mouse pointer to place the imported text.

Do you need to have a text frame on the page to import text into before using the Place command?

Although you can flow text into an existing frame, you do not need to create a frame before importing text.

Topic 4-B

What key do you press as you place text to flow it semi-automatically?

Press Alt as you place text to flow it semi-automatically.

What key do you press as you place text to flow it automatically?

Press Shift as you place text to flow it automatically.

Topic 4-C

Name some advantages of placing text in a multiple-column frame.

You can easily move all of the columns of text at the same time; the gutter cannot be easily changed by inadvertently dragging one column; you can set a fixed column width to quickly add or subtract columns by adjusting the frame width.

Briefly describe how to break a thread to a frame.

Click the prior frame's out port, then click within the frame that you wish to unthread. The text will return to the prior frame, which will then be overset.

When you delete one frame from a threaded series, does the text get deleted as well?

The text that was in the frame you deleted is threaded to the next frame in the series. If you deleted the last frame, the text returns to the out port of the prior frame, waiting to be threaded to another frame.

LESSON REVIEW 5

Topic 5-A

What color model should you use to create colors if you are planning on getting a document commercially printed?

You should use the CMYK color model for documents that will be commercially printed, because the color components match those of the inks that will be used, resulting in a more reliable, predictable color.

When is it best to use the RGB color model?

You should use the RGB color model when preparing documents primarily intended for viewing onscreen, or for outputting to a film recorder.

Topic 5-B

With which palettes can you create a gradient?

You can create a gradient using either the Gradient palette or by choosing New Gradient Swatch from the Swatches palette drop-down list.

How can you add a new color stop to a gradient?

While viewing the gradient bar within the Gradient palette or the New Gradient Swatch palette, click below the gradient bar to add a color stop. Then select the stop and specify its color value.

Topic 5-C

How do you apply a color to the stroke of a frame?

Click the Stroke icon in the Toolbox, the Color palette, or the Swatches palette, and either click a swatch in the Swatches palette, or drag component sliders in the Color palette to create a new stroke color.

How do you ensure that a filled frame bleeds to the edge of a printed page?

Extend the frame a bit past the page edges to ensure that when the paper is trimmed to its final size, the color will extend fully to the paper edge.

Lesson Review 6

Topic 6-A

Name a fast way to change fonts without choosing one from a menu.

Type the beginning of the font name in the Font field of the Character palette or Control palette until the font you want appears.

Why does using autoleading sometimes cause formatting problems?

If one character of a paragraph is set in a larger size than the rest of the type in the paragraph, that line will have larger leading (based on the large character) than the surrounding lines.

Topic 6-B

What are widows and orphans?

Widows are single lines of text at the top of a column, and orphans are single lines at the bottom of a column.

How can you avoid widows and orphans

Select the paragraphs you wish to prevent widows and orphans from occurring in, choose Keep Options from the Paragraph palette drop-down list, check the Keep Lines Together check box, and enter values in the Start and End fields for the minimum number of lines at the start and end of columns.

Topic 6-C

Why is using styles more efficient than manually formatting type?

By creating styles, you can apply several formats at once, rather than one at a time.

Briefly describe the two techniques for creating styles.

You can create a style by first selecting text to base the style on, then clicking the Create New Style button in the appropriate palette (Character Styles or Paragraph Styles). You can also create a style by choosing New Character Style or New Paragraph Style from the appropriate palette's drop-down list, or by holding down Alt as you click the Create New Style button, to open the New Style dialog box to specify its options.

Topic 6-D

When is it important to apply text inset spacing?

You should use text inset spacing to move text away from the edges of frames with colored backgrounds.

How do you specify text inset spacing?

To apply text inset spacing, choose Object→Text Frame Options, then specify insets in the Inset Spacing fields.

Lesson Review 7

Topic 7-A

Why do pictures sometimes appear jagged and blocky when imported into InDesign, and what can you do about it?

InDesign displays a placeholder, or proxy image, that is much lower resolution than the version that will be printed. You can show the image at a high resolution using the Display Performance submenu commands in the Object menu.

Why might you want to create a frame before placing a picture in InDesign?

When creating a template, you might want to designate a position where a graphic should go, but without placing an actual graphic on the page, since it will change with each use of the template. In any document, if you know the shape that the graphic must fit in, it is easy to create a frame to hold the graphic before placing it.

Topic 7-B

How can you specify that text wrap around a graphic?

Select the graphic frame, and in the Text Wrap palette, specify the type of wrap you want to apply.

How can you specify that text wrap around an irregular shape?

Select the graphic frame, and in the Text Wrap palette, select the Wrap Around Object Shape icon.

Topic 7-C

Name one way to move an existing item from one layer to another.

Answers include:

- *Select one or more items that you wish to move to another layer, and drag the dot representing selected items to another layer.*

- *Select one or more items that you wish to move to another layer, choose Edit→Cut, click another layer, and choose Edit→Paste In Place.*

How can you hide a layer's contents?

Either click the eye icon in the Layers palette, or in the Layer Options dialog box, uncheck the Show Layer check box.

Lesson Review 8

Topic 8-A

To which objects can you apply transparency effects in InDesign?

You can apply transparency to all InDesign items, including text, frames, images, and graphics.

How can you adjust an item's transparency in InDesign?

Select the object, then in the Transparency palette, drag the Opacity slider, or type a value into the Opacity field.

Topic 8-B

How can you apply a dynamic drop-shadow effect to text?

Select the text using the Selection tool, choose Object→Drop Shadow, then specify settings in the Drop Shadow dialog box.

What do blending modes control?

Blending modes control how the colors of a foreground item interact with those of background items.

Topic 8-C

Briefly explain what flattening does.

Flattening reduces multiple layers of transparent items to one layer for printing. It breaks down overlapping transparent areas into components that are either vector or raster depending on their complexity.

How can you quickly identify items in a document that will be affected by transparency flattening?

You can preview the areas in your document that will be affected by transparency flattening using the Flattener Preview palette. Choose Window→Output Preview→Flattener. In the Flattener Preview palette's Highlight drop-down list, select the category of items you want to preview. The items described by that category that are affected by transparency flattening will then appear with a red highlight.

LESSON REVIEW 9

Topic 9-A

How do you create an empty table?

Place the insertion point within a text frame, and choose Table→Insert Table. In the Insert Table dialog box, you can then specify the number of columns and rows, as well as the number of header and footer rows.

How do you convert text into a table?

Select the text and choose Table→Convert Text To Table. In the Convert Text To Table dialog box, specify the characters in the text that should indicate where new columns and rows occur.

Topic 9-B

How can you format text within a table?

Select the table cells whose text you want to format, then apply the formatting options just as you would with other InDesign text. To apply a color to the text in selected cells, be sure to first select the Formatting Affects Text button.

How can you apply a color to table cells?

Select the table cells, then apply the color attributes just as you would for other InDesign items.

LESSON 10

Task 10A-1 Page 189

1. **What type of printing combines all of the inks directly onto the finished medium at once and is usually used for low print quantities?**

   Composite printing.

2. **What is the advantage to using a spot color?**

   Spot colors allow you to use a specific color, that won't vary, when a specific color is important. For example, spot colors are sometimes used for a logo. Spot colors are frequently used to save on printing costs; one-, two-, or three-ink printing jobs are less expensive than process color jobs, which use four inks. Many two-ink publications combine a spot color with black, or use two spot colors.

Lesson Review 10

Topic 10-A

What is the main difference between desktop color printing and commercial printing?

Desktop color printers produce composite color pages with all of the ink colors combined, whereas commercial printing is done by creating individual pieces of film for each ink color, which are used to create printing plates for a press.

In terms of the available colors you can print, what is an advantage of commercial printing, as opposed to desktop printing?

An advantage to printing color separations to a commercial press, as opposed to composite color printing on a desktop printer, is that you can add spot colors to the page.

Topic 10-B

Why is it important to maintain the links to placed graphics in your publication?

If a link between your publication and a placed image is missing, it would print at screen resolution (72 ppi), which is too low for professional output.

Name two problems that may be present in your document that the Preflight dialog box does not report as problems.

Possible answers include the following: Your document may use fonts that are available, but that you did not intend to use. The document may require more printing inks than the press can handle in one pass. The printing information reported on may not match those that will actually be used for printing.

Topic 10-C

How do you ensure that a large page will fit on the paper to which you're printing?

Click Setup in the Print dialog box, then select the Scale To Fit option.

How do you add printers marks to a document when you print it?

Click Marks And Bleed in the Print dialog box, then select the printers marks you want to do using the check boxes in the Marks section.

Topic 10-D

What elements does the Package command gather for handoff to a commercial printer?

The Package command gathers all files necessary for printing (the InDesign document and any linked images), and produces a report that contains the information from the Printing Instructions dialog box, as well as detailed information on fonts, colors and inks, links and images, print settings, and a file package list.

When packaging files to send to a commercial printer, how can you include the fonts with the files you package?

In the Package Publication dialog box, check the Copy Fonts (Roman Only) check box.

LESSON REVIEW 11

Topic 11-A

How can you generate bookmarks for an InDesign file you export to PDF?

Select text or another item in the InDesign file, and in the Bookmarks palette, click the New Bookmark button.

What image resolution is good for color and grayscale images in PDF documents intended for the Web?

72 ppi is usually adequate for color and grayscale images in Web PDF documents.

Topic 11-B

Why is it useful to create PDF presets?

PDF presets enable you to change all of the settings in the PDF Export dialog box by choosing one named preset from a menu. If you create PDF files for different purposes (for example, for the Web and for print), it is much faster and possibly more accurate to choose a preset than to change many settings.

Which category of PDF export settings cannot be saved as part of a preset?

Security settings are not available when you create a PDF preset, because those settings are document specific, and PDF presets can be used with any document.

Topic 11-C

What image resolution is good for color and grayscale images in PDF documents intended for desktop printing?

A resolution of 300 ppi is usually adequate for color and grayscale images in PDF documents for printing.

Which PDF preset is appropriate for professional, high-quality printing?

The Press preset.

auto leading
Leading set automatically by InDesign; by default auto leading is set to 120% of the type size.

baseline
The invisible line on which most letters sit.

Bézier shape
A line consisting of points connected by curved or straight segments. A Bézier path may be open or closed.

bleed
When an item extends beyond the page edge, so that when the page is printed on oversized paper and trimmed to size, the item's color will extend to the very edge. InDesign CS allows for separate bleeds on each side of the page of up to 6 inches.

CMYK color
A color model that defines colors by their cyan, magenta, yellow, and black components. CMYK is typically used to define colors for printing, since those are the ink colors used in most printers and presses.

design grid
The combination of margins and guides that helps you structure a document as you design it.

EPS graphic
A graphic saved in the EPS (Encapsulated PostScript) format. EPS files can hold Bézier curve-based (vector) graphics as well as raster images (pixel-based images such as photographic images), and are typically created by applications such as Adobe Photoshop, Adobe Illustrator, Macromedia FreeHand, or CorelDraw.

flattening
A technology that merges overlapping objects that have transparency applied to them into one flat set of opaque objects.

GIF graphic
A graphic saved in the GIF (Graphic Interchange Format) format. GIF files can hold only raster images (pixel-based images such as photographic images) with up to 256 colors, and are typically created by applications such as Adobe Photoshop or web graphics applications.

gradient
A blend between two or more colors.

imagesetter
An output device that generates high-resolution output from a computer file, typically for camera-ready content.

JPEG graphic
A graphic saved in the JPEG (Joint Photographic Experts Group) format. JPEG files can hold only raster images (pixel-based images such as photographic images), and are typically created by applications such as Adobe Photoshop, scanner software, or digital cameras.

LAB color
A color model that defines colors by a luminance (brightness) component, as well as by two chromatic components (green to red balance, and blue to yellow balance). LAB color is typically used for displaying colors on a monitor and for color management software, since it has a wide gamut and is not defined based on any specific device.

leading
The vertical distance between the baselines of two lines of type.

orphan
A single line at the bottom of a column.

process color
A color that is printed by combining cyan, magenta, yellow, and black inks, which are combined during the printing process.

GLOSSARY

raster graphics
Elements composed of an array of pixels.

RGB color
A color model that defines colors by their red, green, and blue components. RGB is typically used for defining colors displayed on screen, since those are the phosphor colors used in monitors.

spot color
A color that is printed using a single ink.

thumbnails
Several reduced-size pages printed per sheet of paper.

TIFF graphic
A graphic saved in the TIFF (Tagged Image File Format) format. TIFF files can hold only raster images (pixel-based images such as photographic images), and are typically created by applications such as Adobe Photoshop or scanner software.

tiling
A large document page printed across several sheets of paper.

vector graphics
Elements composed of mathematically defined shapes.

widow
A single line at the top of a column.

INDEX